PASSWORDS TO POWER

By. Horace L. Patterson

Nashville, Tennessee 37209

PASSWORDS TO POWER

by Dr. Horace L. Patterson

Passwords to Power

Copyright © 2004 by the R. H. Boyd Publishing Corporation

6717 Centennial Blvd.

Nashville, TN 37209-1049

ISBN 1-58942-275-9

All rights reserved. No part of this publication may be reproduced, stored in a retrieval system, or transmitted in any form or by any means, electronic, mechanical, photocopy, recording, or otherwise, without the prior written permission of the copyright owner.

All Scripture quotations are taken from the Holy Bible, *King James Version*.

Printed in the United States of America

Table of Contents

Preface 4

Chapter 1 Shibboleth 5

Chapter 2 Jehovah—Nissi 29

Chapter 3 Jehovah—Shalom 38

Chapter 4 Jehovah—Rapha 48

Chapter 5 Jehovah—Tsidkenu 69

Chapter 6 Jehovah—Shammah 82

Chapter 7 Jehovah—Raah 104

Chapter 8 Jehovah—Jireh 122

Chapter 9 Prayers 136

    I.   Facing the Terrorist of Physical Sickness 136

    II. Facing the Terrorist of Financial Trouble 137

    III. Facing the Terrorist Who Came to Steal Our Peace .138

    IV. Facing the Terrorist Threatening to Our Nation 139

    V.   Facing the Terrorist of Guilt 141

    VI. Facing the Terrorist Spirit of the Antichrist 143

    VII. Facing the Terrorist of Discouragement 144

Chapter 10 Wars, Weapons and Warriors 146

PREFACE

Chapter 1

SHIBBOLETH
Pronounce or Perish

The Book of Judges explains the importance of pronouncing the right words in perilous circumstances.

"And the Gileadites took the passages of Jordan before the Ephraimites; and it was so, that when those Ephraimites: which were escaped said, Let me go over; that the men of Gilead said unto him, Art thou an Ephraimite? If he said, nay; then said they unto him, say now Shibboleth and he said Sibboleth: for he could not frame to pronounce it right. Then they took him, and slew him at the passages of Jordan: and there fell at that time of the Ephraimites forty and two thousand" (Judges 12:5-6).

Forty-two thousand men died at the Jordan river in a disconcerting setup because they could not pronounce the word Shibboleth. Proverbs 18:19 says: "A brother offended is harder to be won than a strong city: and their contentions are like bars of a castle."

Family fights are sometimes the worst fights of all. The Ephraimites contended sharply with Jephthah, the judge, and the men of Gilead. Jephthah was a victim who refused to remain a victim. He was blamed for his father's sin and his mother's profession (Judges 11:1-3). He was not responsible for his birth to a mother who was a prostitute and a father who never married her, yet he was treated with contempt and branded with a misplaced shame. His own brothers threw him out of their family, but God took him in. Whenever we turn to God, we will discover His face, already focused in our direction. Our thoughts of God don't bring God into our lives, but rather it is His thoughts of us that finally strike a responsive chord in our souls. We might love God, but it is not us who loved first and nor is it us who loves best.

Two women have similar circumstances. They both experience an unwanted divorce. As time passes, one says, "I've fallen to pieces." The other resoundingly says, "Free at last. Thank God Almighty I'm free at last." They both experienced the same pain, but each marked the same reality with different measuring rods. One saw the end as the last opportunity for happiness. The other saw the end as a means to give birth to a brand new and far better beginning. The end of one thing is not the end of everything if you know the password to peace and power.

Why Did it Happen to Us on September 11, 2001?

From classrooms to cathedrals all over America, many Americans have asked, "Why us?" As I have brooded over the question, I have found solace in the fact our God is a God of purpose. He truly "writes with a pen that never blots, speaks with a tongue that never slips and acts with a hand that never fails."

On September 11, 2001, God allowed the terrorists to carry out this nightmare because He knew America was strong enough to do something about it. The Taliban had run out of time. Osama bin Laden had run out of mercy. God permitted the strong to suffer in order to release the weak. God allowed America to experience this nightmare in order to end the nightmarish oppression the weak and innocent people of Afghanistan endured each and every day during the rule of the Taliban.

Somebody had been praying for the women of Afghanistan, and we never know how God will answer prayer. The Taliban had created an atrocious climate so evil the women were stoned to death if they were not covered from head to toe in black attire. One woman was publicly stoned to death because her elbow was uncovered. Women were locked away and unable to watch television, listen to the radio, learn to read, or choose a mate. They had no rights, no respect and no recourse for being wronged or raped. Missionaries were arrested, jailed, and threatened with the death penalty for sharing the love and message of salvation through Jesus Christ.

Somebody was praying for the girls who suffered indignities and for the women who could not help them. Somebody was praying for the men who had to grow beards to a certain length or suffer public lashing, imprisonment, and possible death for the absence of facial hair.

God allowed people in America from more than 70 countries to cross over from time to eternity because He was ready to judge the Taliban, defeat Al-Qaeda, and stop Osama bin Laden. The innocent people who died on September 11, 2001, died so others would be treated with dignity and respect.

Just as surely as the Almighty God allowed Pharaoh to harden his heart in ancient Egypt, God allowed Osama bin Laden to mastermind his evil assault because God was tired of his evildoing. Somebody was praying, but, again, we never know how God will answer prayer.

Thousands died so millions might be inspired by God's wisdom and find in all creation the revelation of His glory through Jesus Christ, our Lord. Before bombs were dropped, food was provided to starving people who may have died otherwise. Loved ones left us, but they did not die in vain. Their sacrifices opened our hearts to recommit ourselves to feeding all of God's children based on biblical injunctions of Jesus Christ, our blessed Lord.

The French scientist Louis Pasteur once said, "When I approach a child he inspires me in two sentiments: tenderness for what he is, and respect for what he may become." Our attention is now focused on what the hungry, suffering children of Afghanistan are without the evil Taliban regime and what they can become if given the opportunity. The elderly of that culture who have had to bury sons who were their hopes and daughters who were their hearts have become recipients of our favor because of what we know and feel now. We now know we share a common enemy who can be overcome by God's grace.

There is a sense of loss, but it has given us a greater understanding of family. Because of what happened, we now are bound to our larger human family. We have no choice. We will not neglect the ones our loved ones died to save. God knows what He made us from and how we will respond to what He permits to touch us. This is the language of God. Learn it, and it will bless you as you bless others.

God Knows How To Use Television

For days all we saw on television was the heartbreaking nightmare—the Pentagon in flames and jetliners crashing into U.S. landmarks. The terrorists rejoiced, for they thought the scenes would take our courage. They thought the acts of that day would steal our peace of mind and make us prisoners in our own nation. They thought the rest of the world would choke after learning what happened in the United States of America. They were certain the powers previously opposing them would submit when they saw what could happen to a superpower, but they were wrong. God is always in charge, even when circumstances seem to indicate otherwise. I was a teenager growing up in Bessemer and Birmingham, Alabama, during the early 1960s. As an African-American youth, I was deeply involved in the Civil Rights Movement. I marched in Birmingham when Commissioner Eugene "Bull" Connors gave the command for water hoses and police dogs to be used against us in order to communicate his loathing of us simply because we fought the evils of segregation. I marched on "Bloody Sunday" in Selma, Alabama, when police officers, deputies, and state troopers attacked 600 marchers using tear gas and billy clubs. In each instance, the racist mentality was, "We will show African Americans and the world our superiority."

They were wrong. The television cameras were rolling. The evil that was done to African Americans was shown around the world, and the world said, "This must stop." The world passed judgment, and the verdict was the inferior label did not belong to the victims, but to those who could inflict upon other human beings the evil African Americans suffered. God took the very events designed to destroy us and break our spirits to defeat our enemies. God defeated them with the works of their own hands.

What God did in Birmingham and Selma during the 1960s, He repeated in New York, Pennsylvania, and Washington, D.C. in 2001.

As Americans watched the events of September 11, 2001, God's grace enabled the nation to stand strong instead of becoming fearful. Heroes came forth from all walks of life. Compassion and courage won the day. We wept, and our tears gave birth to a new surge of patriotism. We returned to our spiritual roots. God transformed destruction into construction with the hands of those who hate us. God changed parental concerns raised about television content into family time where we bowed in memory of those who gave us the heritage of rekindled hope. God used television to change into a resource what our enemies felt would leave us limping. We continue to wave our flags and sing "God Bless America."

Those who can interpret the code and speak the language find grace and peace to live through circumstances meant for our demise. What God has done collectively He can do again individually as we face a life that will have "wars and rumors of wars" (Matthew 24:6). Some will be public, and the whole world will know about them. Some will be private, and only you and God will know.

Let us not be deceived. There are contradictions in the human condition. We have a higher side, and we have a lower side. Shakespeare captured this duality revealing our nature in two of his plays.

"What a piece of work is man! how noble in reason! how infinite in faculty! in form and moving how express and admirable! in action how like an angel! in apprehension how like a god!" (Hamlet, 2.2).

"When he is best, he is a little worse than a man and when he is worst, he is little better than a beast" (The Merchant of Venice, 1.2).

As we face the Osama bin Ladens of this world, we must never allow them to make us into what they are. If we choose hatred instead of justice, we will only prove we are as sinful as the sources we seek to replace and defeat. If we allow the violence inflicted upon us to make us into violent people, we will only substitute one form of madness for another. The temptation is great, but we must choose justice over revenge, life over death, and right over wrong. The choice we make will come from the language we speak to ourselves.

It is not a question of whether wars will rage or rumors of wars will be heard. They will. It is not an issue of whether Satan will attack us with another person or all by himself. He'll do both. It's not debatable that even when the spirit is willing the flesh is weak. It is.

The real question before us in the face of so many factors that confront us daily is when Bible study is over and prayer meeting has ended, what will we say to ourselves? When we want to talk about pay and Jesus continues to talk about giving back, what will we say to ourselves? When we are inundated with the task of navigating our way through a world saturated with contrary currents, what will we say to ourselves? When the benediction has been given and the corporate worship experience is over after our hearts have burned because of the message of a living Christ, what will we say to ourselves?

What we say to ourselves determines what we will do and where we will go. What we say to ourselves will limit or spur our success.

Jephthah could have perished in self-pity or self-defeating anger, but he did neither. In this life, we will all experience rejection to some degree. It happens in churches when we give our best, and our labor goes unappreciated by those whose opinions of us are prized highly by us. It happens when our spouses, who promised to be there always for us, seem to have no time for us. Downsizing, financial loss, the unstable market on which we relied, or the children we lovingly raised who call or come by only on the holidays—they each could usher us to the places of devastation and depression.

Some who faithfully attend church go through the motions while carrying weights of care and burden that are heavier than the deeds that were done to them. We make what happens to us a weightier load when we seek help from the resources that can't help. If you are depressed and dejected, a simple compliment from someone doesn't make all the pain pass. You need to pronounce a message about God to yourself. You need to clothe yourself with promises that can't fail.

You need to cover your head with a roof that never leaks and comfort yourself with a companion who will never leave. With the right password, you can defeat the devil's depression and the world's disasters!

Don't be silent when your soul needs to hear a password from God.

"I said, I will take heed to my ways, that I sin not with my tongue: I will keep my mouth with a bridle, while the wicked is before me. I was dumb with silence, I held my peace, even from good; and my sorrow was stirred. My heart was hot within me, while I was musing the fire burned: then spake I with my tongue, Lord, make me to know mine end, and the measure of my days, what it is; that I may know how frail I am. Behold, thou hast made my days as an handbreadth; and mine age is as nothing before thee: verily every man at his best state is altogether vanity" (Psalm 39:1-5).

This psalm has a portion of its roots in the Book of Job and the Book of Ecclesiastes. David, during a downward swirl of events, probably benefited greatly from Job's experience. Sometimes you never truly appreciate a Bible passage until you hit a bump in the road so fiercely you feel you could have written the Scripture yourself.

The major difference between Job and David was one of cause and effect. David had sinned, but Job could not see a cause and effect relationship between sin and his suffering. Job's world began to cave in around him, he sought to live a life of integrity before God. Dissension, disease, and disaster ripped his world to shreds, and he didn't know why. He had no idea his life had become a drama, which Satan struggled to master. In the end, God gave Job double for all he had lost. God even doubled the length of Job's days. He enjoyed another 140 years of blessing and God's favorable benediction.

Unlike Job, David knew he had sinned. He had abused his power, position, and privilege. In Psalm 39, he had reached a point where he resolved to sin no more. David affirmed he would keep silent and endure his sorrows. This was both good and bad. It was good because his enemies could not and would not hear his complaints. There was in David's life a villainous man by the name of Shimei. Shimei was the kind of fellow who enjoyed pouring it on when he caught an adversary down and out.

David was on the run from his son Absalom. The terrifying news spread like wild fire that the king's son had risen up against him. As David and those close to him fled from the city of Jerusalem, they traveled a road leading past the walls of Bahurim. As David approached, one of Saul's relatives verbally and physically assaulted him and his officials (2 Samuel 16:4-8).

Shimei symbolizes a dangerous group of people we face in the war between good and evil. He represents those who have no apprehension about using deceit to destroy. Shimei was wrongly cursing David, and he knew it. David in no way had been slaughtering the household of Saul. In fact it was David, who in a profound gesture, ministered to a grandson of Saul with kingly kindness.

> "And David said, Is there yet any that is left of the house of Saul, that I may show him kindness for Jonathan's sake? And there was of the house of Saul a servant whose name was Ziba. And when they had called him unto David, the king said unto him, Art thou Ziba? And he said, Thy servant is he. And the king said, Is there not yet any of the house of Saul, that I may show the kindness of God unto him? And Ziba said unto the king, Jonathan hath yet a son, which is lame on his feet. And the king said unto him, Where is he? And Ziba said unto the king, behold, he is in the house of Machir, the son of Ammiel, in Lo-debar. Then king David sent, and fetched him out of the house of Machir, the son of Ammiel from Lo-debar. Now when Mephibosheth, the son of Jonathan, the son of Saul, was come unto David, he fell on his face, and did reverence. And David said, Mephibosheth. And he answered, Behold thy servant!
>
> And David said unto him, Fear not: for I will surely show thee kindness for Jonathan thy father's sake, and will restore thee all the land of Saul thy father; and thou shalt eat bread at my table continually. And he bowed himself, and said, What is thy servant, that thou shouldest look upon such a dead dog as I am?

"Then the king called to Ziba, Saul's servant, and said unto him, I have given unto thy master's son all that pertained to Saul and to all his house. Thou therefore, and thy sons and thy servants shall till the land for him, and thou shalt bring in the fruits, that thy master's son may have food to eat; but Mephibosheth thy master's son shall eat bread always at my table. Now Ziba had fifteen sons and 20 servants. Then said Ziba unto the king, According to all that my lord the king hath commanded his servant, so shall thy servant do. As for Mephibosheth, said the king, he shall eat at my table as one of the king's sons. And Mephibosheth had a young son, whose name was Micha. And all that dwelt in the house of Ziba were servants unto Mephibosheth. So Mephibosheth dwelt in Jerusalem for he did eat continually at the king's table; and was lame on both his feet" (2 Samuel 9:1-13).

While David was on the run from Absalom, Ziba the servant of Mephibosheth became a vocal part of David's entourage by the time they passed the walls of Bahurim.

"And when David was a little past the top of the hill, behold, Ziba the servant of Mephibosheth met him, with a couple of asses saddled, and upon them two hundred loaves of bread, and an hundred bunches of raisins, and an hundred of summer fruits, and a bottle of wine. And the king said unto Ziba, What meanest thou by these? And Ziba said, The asses be for the king's household to ride on; and the bread and summer fruit for the young men to eat; and the wine, that such as be faint in the wilderness may drink. And the king said, And where is thy master's son? And Ziba said unto the king, Behold he abideth at Jerusalem: for he said, Today shall the house of Israel restore me the kingdom of my father. Then said the king to Ziba, Behold thine are all that pertained unto Mephibosheth. And Ziba said, I humbly beseech thee that I may find grace in thy sight, my lord, O king" (2 Samuel 16:1-4)

Shimei knew his slanderous words—labeling David as having slaughtered the household of Saul—would effect David deeply but he didn't stop there. His second false assertion proclaimed an open lie against God. Shimei said to David, "The Lord hath delivered the kingdom into the hand of Absalom thy son" (2 Samuel 16:8b). The Lord had not given the kingdom to Absalom. The Bible reveals what actually happened despite Shimei's total disregard for the truth (2 Samuel 15:1-6).

> And it came to pass after this, that Absalom prepared him chariots and horses, and fifty men to run before him. And Absalom rose up early, and stood beside the way of the gate: and it was so, that when any man that had a controversy came to the king for judgment, then Absalom called unto him, and said, Of what city art thou? And he said, thy servant is of one of the tribes of Israel. And Absalom said unto him, See, thy matters are good and right; but there is no man deputed of the king to hear thee. Absalom said moreover, Oh that I were made judge in the land, that every man which hath any suit or cause might come unto me, and I would do him justice! And it was so, that when any man came nigh to him to do him obeisance, he put forth his hand, and took him, and kissed him. And on this manner did Absalom to all Israel that came to the king for judgment: so Absalom stole the hearts of the men of Israel" (2 Samuel 15:1-6).

God had not given Absalom the kingdom, but "he stole the hearts of the men of Israel" (v. 6). Beware of those who seek to steal intangible possessions from you because they are far more important than material goods. Some seek to steal your peace, your passion, and your power. Don't allow them to do so just as David didn't allow Shimei to take what God had given him. Don't allow them to do so just as David didn't permit Absalom to pull down what God had built up.

Absalom's actions hurt David, but it was a hurt that God made him strong enough to live beyond. David was God's man, and he knew God loved him despite his sins. In Psalm 39, David says, "And now Lord, what wait I for? my hope is in thee. Deliver me from all my transgressions: make me not the reproach of the foolish" (vv. 7-8).

David viewed his suffering as chastisement from God. Instead of slapping at the hand of God, David kissed the hand of the Almighty who punished his wrongdoing. When you are a child of God you have a heavenly Father who is committed to being your Father full-time. Even when you no longer want to obey as a child of God should, He never stops being your Father.

David put "and now Lord" on all of his problems (v. 7). If Shimei and Absalom had taken away his roof, he would have covered his head with "and now Lord." If they had pushed him out on a chilly day, he would have come in out of the cold with "and now, Lord." If they had dropped him into a deep and dark pit, he would have climbed up by the never failing light of "and now Lord."

The word *and* means that no matter what the devil and his angels do, they don't have the final word. People don't have the last word. God can always place an *and* where people place a period. When people hurt you, learn to say *and*. When vicious rumors are constructed to destroy your character, learn to say *and*. When your day is dark and your night is long, learn to form your lips to utter *and*. The strongest diseases and most perplexing problems in the economy of humanity are too weak to stand in the presence of God. Your biggest problem is too little to cause God to break a sweat.

The word *and* means something more is to come. There is always something more when we understand that God has inexhaustible riches. You cannot exhaust God. No matter how often He has blessed you in the past and no matter how much your adversaries hate to admit it, there is something more coming. More grace. More mercy. More divine intervention. More deliverance. More miracles. When you are in Christ and Christ is in you, there is always the promise of something more. Learn to pronounce the word *and* as it is fulfilled in the kingdom of God.

> And these three men, Shadrach, Meshach, and Abed-nego, fell down bound into the midst of the burning fiery furnace. Then Nebuchadnezzar the king was astonished, and rose up in haste, and spake, and said unto his counselors, Did not we cast three men bound into the midst of the fire? They answered and said unto the king, True, O king. He answered and said, Lo, I see four

men loose, walking in the midst of the fire, and they have no hurt; and the form of the fourth is like the Son of God (Daniel 3:23-25).

Despite enduring the fire, the Bible makes it clear in verse 25 the Hebrew boys were not harmed.

Learn to say *and* for the word *and* also means "added to, together, or along with." Indeed Shadrach, Meshack, and Abed-nego were in the fire, but added to the fire, together in the fire, and along with them in their midst, was a fourth man–the presence "like the Son of God" (v. 25).

When Lazarus was dead, Jesus showed up "and he that was dead came forth" (John 11:44).

When the Widow of Nain had lost her only son, Jesus showed up, "And he that was dead sat up, and began to speak" (Luke 7:15).

David said, "And now Lord" (Psalm 39:7)

The word *now* means "at the present time." The present (the current time) is always a present (gift) from God. Psalm 46 describes the God of the Bible by saying, "God is our refuge and strength, a very present help in trouble" (v. 1).

All we have is the present. Don't fail to enjoy it. Yesterday is a memory. Tomorrow is a possibility, but today is what you have right now. Be thankful for it, and use it for God's glory. God will automatically use it for your greatest good.

When you read carefully the third chapter of the Book of Daniel you discover three men went into the furnace of fire, but the king saw four men. When the hour of deliverance arrived, only three men left the furnace. The fourth man, the one of whom King Nebuchadnezzar referred to as "like the Son of God," never left. It seems He took up residence in the fire. That's good news for us. He's already in the fire. He's waiting to teach us how to walk in places that destroy others, and He's willing to walk with us as we learn. The Christ we serve is our Maker and our Model.

Through life's troubles and trials, we learn more about the character of God. Job realized, "I have heard of thee by the hearing of the ear; but now mine eye seeth thee" (Job 42:5).

Martha also realized Jesus' power as she grieved the loss for her brother Lazarus. In the face of a promise from Jesus, Martha found the faith to say, "Lord, if thou hadst been here, my brother had not died. But I know, that even now, whatsoever thou wilt ask of God, God will give it thee"(John 11:21-22).

In spite of dismal doubts, Martha refused to pronounce total defeat because she realized God could change the situation *now*.

Fears and a host of obstacles mount against us all, but we can rise above the assaults of evil if we always remember our God is the God of now. His deity is not relegated to the dim and distant past. He is, of course, the God of Abraham, Isaac, and Jacob, as well as of Sarah, Rebekah, and Rachel. Praises be to Him because He is also the God of now! Say it. Believe it. Pronounce it. Repeat it. Remember it. If necessary, reclaim it and resolve to never ever forget it again.

David said, "And now Lord" (Psalm 39:7).

The Hebrew word for Lord used in this passage is Adonai. It means "master or ruler," and it refers to God's right to rule over us. You can't call him Lord and say no to Him. If you call Him Master, then you have no right to respond negatively. As Lord, He has the right to make all of the important decisions in your life. As Lord, He claims our love, our lives, and our loyalty. As Lord, He can never be told no, for He cannot be Lord where He does not rule.

When Shimei attacked David with words and rocks, David's bodyguard, Abishai, spoke up. "Then said Abishai the son of Zeruiah unto the king, Why should this dead dog curse my lord the king? Let me go over, I pray thee, and take off his head" (2 Samuel 16:9). He wanted to fight David's enemy with physical weapons.

When you truly learn the language of God, you quickly learn you can't fix all of your problems with any weapon—guns, knives, words, and so forth—unless it is the "sword of the Spirit, which is the word of God" (Ephesians 6:17). You can't go through this life attempting to cut up and cut off your troubles. Be mindful for every Shimei who attacks you, there is a corresponding Abishai just waiting, willing, and able to seek some form of revenge. Abishai said, "Let me go over." David said "Let him alone" (v. 11).

"And David said to Abishai, and to all his servants, Behold, my son, which came forth of my bowels, seeketh my life: how much more now may this Benjamite do it? Let him alone, and let him curse; for the Lord hath bidden him. It may be that the Lord will look on mine affliction, and that the Lord will requite me good for his cursing this day. And as David and his men went by the way, Shimei went along on the hill's side over against him, and cursed as he went, and threw stones at him, and cast dust. And the king, and all the people that were with him, came weary, and refreshed themselves there" (2 Samuel 16:11-14).

When you begin to speak God's language, you will fall out of step with the way the world resolves conflict. As a matter of fact, we become to the world "fools for Christ's sake" (1 Corinthians 4:10). David told Abishai that "the Lord" had told Shimei to curse him.

What a great thought! Sometimes God allows people to curse you for one simple reason—so He can give you good for their cursing (1 Samuel 16:12). If you allow God to stretch you, you will become too big to be little enough to take revenge.

As I share these thoughts my mind races back to July of 1965. I preached my first sermon at my membership church, New Saint Paul in Bessemer, Alabama. My subject was "God Can Change Things." I had no idea how prophetic that message would prove to be in my life and in the lives of many people whom I've served as pastor and in my professional career as an administrator, educator, elected official, and author. I can attest God can change challenging circumstances into a living witness of His amazing grace to an unbelieving world.

It didn't take long for Absalom's army to be defeated. Absalom's mule went under the thick branches of a large oak tree. His head got caught in the tree, and he was left hanging as the mule continued without him (2 Samuel 18:9). David, after a period of mourning, returned to Jerusalem to reclaim his throne.

"And he bowed the heart of all the men of Judah, even as the heart of one man; so that they sent this word unto the king, Return thou, and all thy servants. So the king returned, and came to Jordan. And Judah came to Gilgal, to go to meet the king, to conduct the king over Jordan. And Shimei the son of Gera, a Benjamite, which was of Bahurim, hasted and came down with the men of Judah to meet king David. And there were a thousand men of Benjamin with him, and Ziba the servant of the house of Saul, and his fifteen sons and his twenty servants with him; and they went over Jordan before the king. And there went over a ferry boat to carry over the king's household, and to do what he thought good. And Shimei the son of Gera fell down before the king, as he was come over Jordan. And said unto the king, Let not my lord impute iniquity unto me, neither do thou remember that which thy servant did perversely the day that my lord the king went out of Jerusalem, that the king should take it to his heart. For thy servant doth know that I have sinned: therefore, behold, I am come the first this day of all the house of Joseph to go down to meet my lord the king. But Abishai the son of Zeruiah answered and said, Shall not Shimei be put to death for this, because he cursed the Lord's anointed? And David said, What have I to do with you, ye sons of Zeruiah, that ye should this day be adversaries unto me? shall there any man be put to death this day in Israel? for do not I know that I am this day king over Israel? Therefore the king said unto Shimei, thou shalt not die. And the king sware unto him" (2 Samuel 19:14-23).

Shimei became desperate to make things right. He had milked David's vulnerability. Things had changed because God had moved. Absalom was gone, and David was back on top. The people shouted for joy and the whole land began to bristle because of the power God had reissued to David. Fear caught Shimei by the throat and dragged out of his evil speaking mouth a pitiful apology by which he hoped to save his life. Abishai had not changed. He, like the New Testament apostle Peter, seems to have been prone to keep his blade sharp just in case. David once again said no to Abishai's request to kill Shimei.

Most people have encountered a Shimei in their lifetime. Those who haven't shouldn't panic, but prepare instead. Sooner or later, you will be greeted by a stone-throwing Shimei. By God's grace, you can overcome any enemy. When you speak God's language, you will come out on top. "And now Lord" is the key to victory despite what precedes it. When people have written you off, don't be bitter. Pronounce "And now Lord" and walk in victory.

When your job has been taken: "'And now Lord,' give me another better than the other." When your child is in trouble "'And now Lord' protect, pronounce, and preserve."

After adversaries have cast their stones and demons have taken their best shot, it's not over if you can just say in your heart, "And now Lord." When friends turn on you, pronounce, "'And now Lord,' be my friend."

Just say it, believe it, and pronounce it. Three words? Yes. But these three words are passwords. They are God's Shibboleth for any person or circumstance that seeks to harm you. AND NOW LORD!

If others kill you with words, they can't stop you. If others try to keep you bound with the sins of the past, realize they can't hold you if you can say with faith, and hope, "And now Lord."

In every area of our lives, God is longing to intervene regardless of our fears. A servant of Abraham was sent on a mission to find a wife for Isaac. He faced a difficult assignment that might have intimidated him, however, he turned to God and joyfully said,

> "And I bowed down my head and worshiped the Lord, and blessed the Lord God of my master Abraham, which had led me in the right way to take my master's brother's daughter unto his son" (Genesis 24:48).

The servant previously had prayed and asked God for Isaac's future bride to meet him at the well, respond favorably when asked to draw water from the well to quench his thirst, and volunteer to draw water to quench the thirst of the ten camels traveling with him. God, who was more than ready to help, went to work before he said, "amen."

> "And it came to pass, before he had done speaking, that, behold, Rebekah came out" (Genesis 24:15a). She was "the daughter of Abraham's brother." After meeting the servant at the well, Rebekah said, "Drink, my lord, and she hasted, and let down her pitcher upon her hand, and gave him drink. And when she had done giving him drink, she said, I will draw water for thy camels also, until they have done drinking" (Genesis 24:18-19).

A camel will drink about five gallons of water. The man had ten. She had the health, will, and strength to draw nearly fifty gallons of water or more. Rebekah didn't know the servant was praying, and he didn't know she was coming. Rebekah didn't know who he was, and he didn't know who she was. He didn't know she wasn't married, and she didn't know he was on an errand to find a bride. In His sovereignty and amazing grace, God brought them together, and he started working as the servant prayed.

God loves to help those in need of help. He is always ready, willing, and able to help those in need. When we lose sight of this, we risk losing battles we ought to be winning.

> "And Asa in the thirty and ninth year of his reign was diseased in his feet, until his disease was exceeding great; yet in his disease he sought not to the Lord, but to the physicians. And Asa slept with his fathers, and died in the one and fortieth year of his reign" (2 Chronicles 16:12-13).

The historian who recorded this simple matter suggested that Asa died when it was possible for him to live because "in his disease he sought not to the Lord, but to the physician (v. 12). There is no condemnation for Asa's reliance on his physicians. The problem was he relied upon them only. No problem is too hard for God, and no concern is too small for His divine attention and intervention. You never worry God when you seek Him about the cares that worry you. Pills plus prayer works, medication plus meditation works, and worship can bring about miracles. Say a prayer and take your pills.

Revisiting the Book of Judges, we don't know all of the details that chartered the course of Jephthah's faith.

"Jephthah uttered all his words before the Lord in Mizpeh" (Judges 11:11). Whatever we do or say always occurs in the presence of the Lord, even though we often forget He hears and sees everything we do. Jephthah spoke as sincerely and as well as he knew how to speak in the presence of God. Mizpeh, known as a natural watch-tower, was Jephthah's home. In simple language, he took his words, his vows, and his desires to his home. Home is where the real you lives. Home is the address of no pretense. Whoever you are at home is who you really are. Just like you can't be a pig and a puppy, you can't be God's real deal unless you're real at home.

Jephthah turned to God already who was turned toward his direction. God became his career counselor and his career partner. He went out as a military leader to face Israel's common enemy—the Ammonites and Jephthah enjoyed a huge victory when God delivered the enemy into his hands. His celebration was short-lived. The Ephraimites resented the status God had given him. The Bible says,

"And the men of Ephraim gathered themselves together, and went northward, and said unto Jephthah, Wherefore passedst thou over to fight against the children of Ammon, and didst not call us to go with thee? We will burn thine house upon thee with fire" (Judges 12:1).

God's blessings are sometimes costly because we live in a fallen world. Sometimes people who should rejoice with you when you rejoice will be envious instead. When it happens, don't lose heart. You don't need everybody's well wishes in order to be victorious. God will prepare a table before you in the presence of your enemies (Psalm 23:5).

Hungry for a Fight

Jephthah and the men of Ephraim should have been close. They were descendants of two brothers born to the patriarch, Joseph, in Egypt. Jephthah was a member of the tribe of Manasseh. Ephraim and Manasseh were sons of Joseph, who possibly was the most forgiving person in the Old Testament. Joseph named his firstborn son Manasseh, which meant God had caused him to "forget all my toil" (Genesis 41:51). Joseph called his second son Ephraim, because God had caused him to be fruitful in Egypt (Genesis 41:52). Two brother's descendants should have been close, but they weren't. "A brother offended is harder to be won than a strong city" (Proverbs 18:19a).

Hungry for a fight, the men of Ephraim spoke harshly to Jephthah saying, "When you fought the Ammonites why didn't you call us to go with you?" Jephthah reminded them that when he called them, they didn't answer or send help. When he saw their apathy he went out to battle, and the Lord delivered the Ammonites into his hands." The Ephraimites' rage had no cause for existence. They had their chance, but they didn't take advantage of the opportunity given. In the economy of God, those who are not faithful with a little cannot be trusted with much. Some never get the next blessing because they didn't make the most of the blessing they already had.

People who are hungry to start a fight seldom win in the end. The Gileadites defeated the men of Ephraim and seized the shallow crossing of the Jordan River leading to Ephraim.

The Test

The men of Ephraim looked like the men of Gilead. Their dress was similar. Facial features, foot speed, height, weight, and gestures all proved to be unreliable indicators to distinguish friend from foe. When a war is going on, you are in a terrible dilemma when you can't discern the enemy. It was hard to tell who was who. I hate to admit it but sometimes when you look at the way some "church folk" act in the world, it's hard to tell they've got their name on a church roll. When you hear the way some people complain and worry, it's hard to know if they own a Bible or even believe when it says, "Fret not thyself because of evildoers, neither be thou envious against the workers of iniquity" (Psalm 37:1).

A war was going on! The men of Gilead found it hard to distinguish the difference between a comrade and an enemy. It was dangerous to trust the wrong man. In order to lower the danger quotient, Jephthah chose a password. It was a simple test that worked with great success. He instructed the Gileadites to have all survivors wanting to cross the Jordan into Ephraim to pronounce the word "Shibboleth." Those who could not pronounce the word would be killed. The men of Ephraim couldn't pronounce the word because it contained a consonant which was not in the Ephraimite dialect. Unable to put the "h" in Shibboleth, they pronounced the word "sibboleth." Forty-two thousand men lost their lives because they could not pronounce the word "Shibboleth."

The men of Ephraim should have been able to say Shibboleth because the word means stream of water. God had been busy revealing His power in their history, yet this entire tribe had so distanced itself from its spiritual roots that they began to speak their own language rather than the language of God.

There are many ways to go "into a far country" away from the familiar presence of God (Luke 15:13). The tribe of Ephraim lost its spiritual balance. The people coveted Jephthah's victory and called it assertiveness training. They polluted the banks of the Jordan with vulgar threats and called it freedom of speech. You don't have to move from Portland to Paris or from Mississippi to Mexico to go to a far country. You can so distance yourself from the bridges that brought you that you don't even resemble the man or woman who once crossed them. You can so neglect the language of faith that you can no longer use it when you need it.

The men of Ephraim should have been able to pronounce the word "Shibboleth." They should have never allowed themselves to assimilate to any dialect that did not afford them an accurate pronouncement of the events that depicted God's mighty hand in their history. A stream of water—"Shibboleth"—should have evoked strong emotions. At the Red Sea, God made a highway, and their foreparents crossed over on dry land (Exodus 14:29). In the wilderness when the people ran out of water, God brought a Shibboleth—a stream of water from a rock in Horeb (Exodus 17:6).

At a place called Marah on their journey to the Promised Land, the people ran into a Shibboleth—a stream of bitter water. God intervened. He showed Moses a special tree, and when the limbs from the tree hit the water, the stream of bitter water was made sweet (Exodus 15:22-23).

On the banks of the Jordan River, the nation of Israel stood with a wishful eye, surveying from a distance their future home. They desired their Promised Land, but they were caught on the wrong side of the river. They had thoughts of a home where they would have a place of shelter and protection, of rest and healing, of warmth and hospitality, but they had one difficult circumstance. The banks of the river overflowed. They had no ships to navigate the deep places of the Jordan. They had no boats to cross over to the home they envisioned on the other side, yet God intervened. When the priests who carried the ark stepped into the overflowing waters, the water stopped flowing and the ground dried up. The nation crossed over. At God's mandate they removed 12 stones from the midst of the river before the miracle concluded. On the banks of the river they set up the 12 stones to commemorate what God had done.

"And it came to pass, when all the people were clean passed over Jordan, that the Lord spake unto Joshua, saying, Take you twelve men out of the people, out of every tribe a man, And command ye them, saying, Take you hence out of the midst of Jordan, out of the place where the priests feet stood firm, twelve stones, and ye shall carry them over with you, and leave them in the lodging place where ye shall lodge this night. Then Joshua called the twelve men, whom he had prepared of the children of Israel, out of every tribe a man: And Joshua said unto them, Pass over before the ark of the Lord your God into the midst of Jordan, and take you up every man of you a stone upon his shoulder, according unto the number of the tribes of the children of Israel: That this may be a sign among you, that when your children ask their fathers in time to come, saying, What mean ye by these stones? Then ye shall answer them, That the waters of Jordan were cut off before the ark of the covenant of the Lord; when it passed over Jordan, the waters of Jordan were cut off: and these stones shall be for a memorial unto the children of Israel for ever. And the children of Israel did so as Joshua commanded, and took up twelve stones out of the midst of Jordan, as the Lord spake unto Joshua, according to the number of the tribes of the children of Israel, and carried them over with them unto the place where they lodged, and laid them down there" (Joshua 4:1-8).

God did not say that the 12 stones would be a memorial for the present generation; He said it would be a memorial forever. He did not say for the next generation only, but forever.

The memorial of God's mighty act of parting waters of the Jordan was designed to be a memorial forever. Yet in the Book of Judges, the men of Ephraim were so divorced from their history, so disconnected from their past, they could not even pronounce the word "Shibboleth," let alone rehearse their history. They had become so distant from their roots they could not even pronounce a word that was saturated with the redemptive acts of the Almighty God. At shibboleth after shibboleth, stream after stream, water obstacle after water obstacle, God had shown His power and revealed His heart. God had been merciful, faithful, and yet the men of Ephraim said "sibboleth."

Imagine a native born adult American who can't pronounce the words "Declaration of Independence," "freedom," or "flag." Imagine an America 20 years from now where there are 42,000 adult soldiers who can't pronounce "Pentagon," "New York," "World Trade Center," or "terrorist." How sad it would be, but sadder still would be the rising up of a generation that could not truly pronounce "Jesus Christ," the Savior who keeps us from hatred and sin's destruction; the Friend who comforts us in sorrow; the Redeemer who promises to give us eternal life; the Light of the World who keeps us from stumbling in dark and dangerous places; and the Presence who is with us through all life's difficulties.

Today, there is a war going on just as there was a war waged between the men of Ephraim and Jephthah and the men of Gilead. It is a war between good and evil. Highjacked airplanes transformed into missiles of murder, tall buildings reduced to rubble, and anthrax in the mail are all visible signs of an invisible war that is older than the planet earth. The apostle Paul explains this in his letter to the Ephesian church by saying,

> "For we wrestle not against flesh and blood, but against principalities, against powers, against the rulers of the darkness of this world, against spiritual wickedness in high places" (Ephesians 6:12).

Let no one be deceived. The war is real. The enemy is vicious. The stakes are high. The tactics are many. The warriors are diverse. They come in all sizes, races, genders, ages, and shapes. There are impostors who seek to befriend you in order to destroy you, but take heart. On that river bank in ancient Israel, although many fell, there were true Gileadites who made it safely through the war zone. When asked for the password they said, "Shibboleth" and passed through where others perished. They knew the password, and they knew how to pronounce the word that represented the hand of God in their history.

A knowledge of the hand of God in our yesterdays give us strength to face uncertain tomorrows with the deep conviction that good will prevail.

A small boy went to school on the day following the night the family's house burned down. A concerned teacher approached him saying, "I am so sorry that your home burned down." The boy looked up and said with the conviction of the convinced, "Thank you for caring but we still have a home. We just don't have a house, right now, to put it in." He went through what caused others to panic. In the pages that follow you will find some passwords that will allow you to soar through what some sink under.

"A thousand shall fall at thy side, and ten thousands at thy right hand; but it shall not come nigh thee. Only with thine eyes shalt thou behold and see the reward of the wicked. Because thou hast made the Lord, which is my refuge, even the most High, thy habitation; there shall no evil befall thee, neither shall any plague come nigh thy dwelling. For he shall give his angels charge over thee to keep thee in all thy ways" (Psalm 91:7-11).

There might be times when we will not have houses in which to reside but through Jesus Christ our Lord, we will always have a home if we can speak the language of God. Every word we learn to speak will give hope another breath because it is the language of God that "brings news of a door that opens at the end of every corridor."

"The work of God in Philadelphia" is what they called "the great city-wide revival campaign of 1858." It was led by a 29-year-old Episcopalian minister by the name of Dudley Tyng. On a Wednesday, Tyng took a break from his sermon preparation time. He went to see a new corn-shelling apparatus. While observing it he moved too closely to it. A sleeve of his coat got caught and his arm was literally torn from his shoulder.

Every effort to save his life failed. Before he left his body for heaven, he whispered a word to his father. He said, "Tell the people to stand up for Jesus." The Presbyterian minister, George Duffield Jr., overheard the whisper. He was so inspired he preached a sermon on the last words of Reverend Tyng and concluded the message with a poem he wrote. A member of the church had the poem printed on leaflets. Someone sent one of the leaflets to a Baptist periodical. The song inspired by a young minister's dying words became a hymn that has blessed thousands because there is a door that opens at the end of every corridor. The hymn was:

Stand up, stand up for Jesus

Ye soldiers of the cross

Lift high His royal banner

It must suffer loss:

From vict'ry unto vict'ry

His army shall He lead when

Every foe is vanquished

And Christ is Lord indeed.

Chapter 2

AND NOW LORD
Pronounce Him as Jehovah-Nissi

The Lord Is Our Banner
(Exodus 17:15)

What we do after a battle is over speaks volumes about the kind of person or people we are. When the pressure is off and the danger is behind, the language of God grows rather than diminishes in importance. Trouble humbles even the most proud people because it brings us face to face with our limitations. Trouble makes demands upon us that none can ignore. Battles have a way of blessing us with gifts we would rarely collect for ourselves because they make us more receptive to heavenly assistance.

> "Before I was afflicted I went astray; but now have I kept thy word. Thou art good, and doest good, teach me thy statutes. The proud have forged a lie against me: but I will keep thy precepts with my whole heart. Their heart is as fat as grease; but I delight in thy law. It is good for me that I have been afflicted; that I might learn thy statutes" (Psalm 119:67-71).

King Uzziah was so great a leader that the prophet Isaiah and most of his nation did not even seek the Lord until King Uzziah died (Isaiah 6:1). Blessed by God with so many victories in his hours of weakness, the king became a national hero. He knew how to speak the language of God as his strong tower in battle (2 Chronicles 26:5-6a).

"And he sought God in the days of Zechariah, who had understanding in the visions of God: and as long as he sought the Lord, God made him to prosper. And he went forth and warred against the Philistines, and brake down the wall of Gath." (Gath was the headquarters of the Philistines). "And God helped him against the Philistines, and against the Arabians." And the Ammonites gave gifts to Uzziah; and his name spread abroad even to the entering in of Egypt" (vv. 8a).

"Moreover Uzziah built towers in Jerusalem…Also he built towers in the desert and digged many wells for he had much cattle…vine dressers in the mountains…for he loved husbandry" (vv. 9a, 10a, 10c).

"Moreover Uzziah had an host of fighting men" (v. 11).

Uzziah had the best weapons. With God's help he had it made. But take notice of verses 15 and 16:

"And he made in Jerusalem engines, invented by cunning men, to be on the towers and upon the bulwarks, to shoot arrows and great stones withal. And his name spread far abroad; for he was marvelously helped, till he was strong. But when he was strong, his heart was lifted up to his destruction: for he transgressed against the Lord his God, and went into the temple of the Lord to burn incense upon the altar of incense."

It was a costly transgression. The war was over. The victories had been won. The reputation had been made. The pressure was off. The word of God informs us of the outcome that always happens when the victor ceases to speak the language of the source of the victory. Second Chronicles 26:17-21 says:

"And Azariah the priest went in after him, and with him fourscore priests of the Lord, that were valiant men: And they withstood Uzziah the king, and said unto him, It appertaineth not unto thee, Uzziah, to burn incense unto the Lord, but to the priests the sons of Aaron, that are consecrated to burn incense: go out of the sanctuary; for thou hast trespassed; neither shall it be for thine honour from the Lord God. Then Uzziah was wroth, and had a censer in his hand to burn incense: and while he was wroth with the priests, the leprosy even rose up in his forehead before the priests in the house of the Lord, from beside the incense altar. And Azariah the chief priest, and all the priests, looked upon him, and, behold, he was leprous in his forehead, and they thrust him out from thence; yea, himself hasted also to go out, because the Lord had smitten him. And Uzziah the king was a leper unto the day of his death, and dwelt in a several house, being a leper; for he was cut off from the house of the Lord: and Jotham his son was over the king's house, judging the people of the land."

When the war was over Moses said, "The Lord is our flag."

Unlike King Uzziah, Moses knew how to handle success. For every person who is defeated by adversity, a hundred others are crushed by success. After the defeat of the Amalekites the Bible says in Exodus 17:14-15:

"And the Lord said unto Moses, Write this for a memorial in a book, and rehearse it in the ears of Joshua: for I will utterly put out the remembrance of Amalek from under heaven. And Moses built an altar, and called the name of it Jehovah-nissi."

Some translations of the phrase "Jehovah-Nissi" read, "The Lord is my Banner." The war was over. The enemy had been overwhelmed. There were no arrows falling from the sky. There were no spears splitting the air with harmful accuracy. There were no calvary charges from the scores of mounted enemy horsemen. The battle was over, but Moses did not relegate God as the flag that was, but as the One who is. The pressure was off, and what you do when the pressure is off is what you do most of the time.

God is so merciful to give us more good days than bad days. Moses had spent the day raising his hands in prayer to the point of weariness; to pray longer required more strength than he had. His hands grew heavy. Aaron and Hur put a stone under him and held up his hands. When his hands were lifted, Israel prevailed, but when he, due to fatigue, let them down, Amalek prevailed. When there is a need that confronts us that we cannot meet due to a lack of our strength and resources, we turn to prayer as naturally as a bird turns to flying or a fish turns to swimming.

Moses built an altar and called it Jehovah-Nissi, which means "the Lord is our Banner." Research indicates flags of metal existed 3,000 years before the birth of Christ. Those flags were made of metal and some designs were shown on ancient Greek coins, Egyptian tombs, and early paintings.

There is something in the human spirit that is aroused by the symbol and language of a flag. A flag represents presence, power, origin, glory, beliefs, and aspirations. A flag can threaten and promise, warn and encourage. A flag represents participation in a community of ideas or fellowship that spans time and distance.

The war against Osama bin Laden and the Taliban will end, but there will always be another war until Jesus returns.

The Taliban will be defeated. Osama bin Laden will be judged as surely as Pharaoh was judged at the Red Sea. Church attendance increases during a crisis. People buy Bibles during a period of chaos because the human soul needs the reassurance that comes only from Scripture.

> "Let not your heart be troubled: ye believe in God, believe also in me. In my Father's house are many mansions: if it were not so, I would have told you. I go to prepare a place for you. And if I go and prepare a place for you, I will come again, and receive you unto myself; that where I am, there ye may be also" (John 14:1-3).

> "The Lord is my shepherd; I shall not want. He maketh me to lie down in green pastures: he leadeth me beside the still waters. He restoreth my soul: he leadeth me in the paths of righteousness for his name's sake. Yea, though I walk through the valley of the shadows of death, I will fear no evil: for thou art with me; thy rod and thy staff they comfort me. Thou preparest a table before me in the presence of mine enemies: thou anointest my head with oil; my cup runneth over. Surely goodness and mercy shall

follow me all the days of my life: and I will dwell in the house of the Lord for ever" (Psalm 23:1-6).

"God is our refuge and strength, a very present help in trouble. Therefore will not we fear, though the earth be removed, and though the mountains be carried into the midst of the sea; Though the waters thereof roar and be troubled, though the mountains shake with the swelling thereof. Selah. There is a river, the streams whereof shall make glad the city of God, the holy place of the tabernacles of the most High. God is in the midst of her; she shall not be moved: God shall help her, and that right early. The heathen raged, the kingdoms were moved: he uttered his voice, the earth melted. The Lord of hosts is with us; the God of Jacob is our refuge. Selah. Come, behold the works of the Lord, what desolations he hath made in the earth. He maketh wars to cease unto the end of the earth; he breaketh the bow, and cutteth the spear in sunder; he burneth the chariot in the fire. Be still, and know that I am God. I will be exalted among the heathen, I will be exalted in the earth. The Lord of hosts is with us; the God of Jacob is our refuge. Selah" (Psalm 46:1-11).

The war will end, but after the terrorist training camps in Afghanistan are destroyed, will you favor Uzziah or Moses?

After the hate-filled voice of Osama bin Laden has been hushed, will you build an altar in your soul and call it Jehovah-Nissi, or will you tuck away the God who is and live as though He is the God who was?

The residents of the city of Kabul, Afghanistan, will bring out their radios and play music in the streets after five years of cruel Taliban treatment is behind, but will you sing unto the Lord a new song at that holy altar in your soul?

After the smoke clears from Ground Zero and a cascade of events turn the evil ones out, will you take it as a matter of fact or as a matter of God?

It would be a massive mistake to fail to pronounce in our souls the language that informs, reminds, and empowers. It would be foolish for us to confine the God who is to a compartment that will never be occupied as the God who was because the need for God is an unchanging need regardless of how the wind blows.

There is an insightful story about a scorpion and a turtle. The scorpion needed to cross the river, but it could not swim. It had to convince a turtle to ferry it across. The turtle's first response was, "No way. You'll sting me, I won't be able to swim, and then I'll drown."

The scorpion assured the turtle that it had nothing to fear. He said, "Don't worry, I'll behave. Besides it wouldn't make any sense for me to sting you. You must be forgetting the fact that I can't swim. If you were to drown, I would drown as well."

The turtle finally conceded and agreed to take the scorpion across the river. Halfway across, the scorpion stung the turtle in the neck. Paralyzed, the turtle cried out, "Why in the world did you do that?" The scorpion replied, "I really don't know. I guess I just couldn't help myself. It's just my nature."

Regardless of time and place, it is just the nature of evil to wage war on goodness. If we fail to speak the words that relate to the abiding fact and unchanged reality of Jehovah-Nissi, we might be Christians in our heads, but we'll become atheists in our practice. We are each challenged to monitor our own internal dialogue with God's message, "Fear not: for they that be with us are more than they that be with them" (2 Kings 6:16).

In both our personal and national battles we need to understand the sum total of intentional and unintentional messages we receive from family, friends, and others who affect us. However, we have a large amount of choice to determine their lasting meaning. Our worth in and out of battle is not determined by the scrimmages we win or lose. Our worth to our God is not meant to be some kind of paint-job others do to us. The Lord is our banner. The Lord is our present reason for going, coming, working, and waiting. In conclusion to *Walden; or, Life in the Woods*, Henry David Thoreau wrote, "If a man does not keep pace with his companions, perhaps it is because he hears a different drummer. Let him step to the music which he hears however measured or far away."

God is our substance and our holy symbol. He is our flag reminding us that we are never alone and never defeated if we appropriate Him as the source of our hope and the firmness of our confidence. Our assets are always greater than our liabilities "because he that is in you is greater, than he that is in the world" (1 John 4:4b).

Regardless of who is in the White House or on the battlefield, God is always on the throne. We must never suffer any creature to be His rival. In his infinite perfection, He will amaze us if we refuse to allow our vision to be blurred of Him who is the banner that never falls to the ground.

In 2 Kings 6, a Syrian army advanced against the prophet Elisha in the city of Dothan. Iron chariots stood in rows ready for battle. Seasoned soldiers gripped the tools of their trade prepared for hostile contact.

In the face of the fight between good and evil we quickly learn man always makes a poor god, but a man or woman in the hands of Almighty God confronts no journey that is too long or too deep a chasm.

The city of Dothan is referred to only twice in the Bible. Joseph met his brothers there, and it was in Dothan he was stripped of his coat of many colors, cast into a dry, dark, and dangerous pit, and later sold into slavery (Genesis 37). It was in this same city Elisha the prophet was surrounded by heavenly chariots of fire (2 Kings 6:17).

God chose not to intervene militarily. He could have smitten Joseph's brothers with blindness as He smote the entire Syrian army at the request of Elisha (2 Kings 6:18). God could have sent a spirit of confusion over Joseph's brothers and "set every man's sword against his fellow" (Judges 7:22) as He did between the Midianites and Amalekites during the days of Gideon (Judges 7).

Some time ago my family went through a very difficult time. One of my sons was unjustly accused by a female teenager of harassment. It was a lie. We knew it from the beginning. We secured a strong legal defense team headed by my nephew attorney Clarence Dortch III, but I knew talent means little in the face of satanic evil. I knew the shortest distance between our crisis and our victory was not the distance between the law offices of our attorneys but the distance between our knees as a family and the floors in our home. We prayed often. We prayed collectively, and we prayed individually. Others prayed with us and for us.

As we neared the date of the trial, the Holy Spirit began to make intercession for me in a way I had not known before. The Holy Spirit also instructed me to pray God would send a spirit of confusion to the accuser and reveal her evil clearly before the judge and entire court to resolve all doubt concerning her truthfulness. God heard. God answered. The lies from her own mouth contradicted themselves. Through her own lips she revealed herself to be untruthful, unethical, and unstable.

God can confuse your enemies and make them testify against themselves. The chariots of fire surrounded Dothan, but God used the evil that happened for good. Years after Joseph's painful ordeal, he told his brothers,

"But as for you, ye thought evil against me; but God meant it unto good, to bring to pass, as it is this day, to save much people alive" (Genesis 50:20).

Every Dothan, every place of conflict, every city of conspirators, every place of pain, every station of sorrow, and every moment of misery is already surrounded by chariots of fire. I don't know how God will use those chariots on your behalf, but child of God, I promise you He will use them with your best interest at heart. God will use those chariots, sometimes immediately, sometimes later to bring to pass certain matters—always to bless you, protect you, and promote you.

Never give in. Never give up. Never cave under. You're in a fight, in a war, but if you keep your eyes on the flag, you'll see for yourself that it never falls to the ground. Put some "and now Lord" on your battlefield. The Lord informs us there is a day coming for the faithful, and in that day He says, "Ye shall ask me nothing" (John 16:23). One day all questions will be answered; God has never wronged any of us. At that day we will have no complaints, no protests, and no resentments. As the hymn is titled, "We'll Understand It Better By and By."

Jehovah-Nissi. Pronounce it, say it, remember it, and live by it daily.

---

[1]Charles R. Swindoll, "David, A Man of Passion and Destiny," Word Publishing, Dallas-London; Vancouver, Melbourne, p. 65.

[2]Charles Allen, "The Touch of the Mater's Hand," Fleming H. Revell Company, Old Tappan, New-Jersey, p. 23.

Chapter 3

And Now Lord
Pronounce Him as Jehovah-Shalom

The Lord Is Our Peace
(Judges 6:24)

"Then Gideon built an altar there unto the Lord, and called it Jehovah-shalom: unto this day it is yet in Ophrah of the Abiezrites" (Judges 6:24).

Faced with what he thought was certain death, Gideon panicked. He had seen an angel of the Lord face to face and was scared because people of Israel believed no one could see God and live.

The Lord said to Moses, "and He said, thou canst not see my face: for there shall no man see me, and live" (Exodus 33:20). But God told Gideon not to be afraid.

In His mercy God had revealed Himself to Gideon through the form of an angel. The situation in Gideon's world was grim. Enemies controlled commerce. Alien armies raided the land at will. The people of God had no punch in their prayers. The high cost of low living had become an invoice that demanded a present payment. The people had lost contact with the Owner whose acreage and sphere of influence was far greater than that of earthly kings. God intervened, however, and in the form of an angel spoke a word of peace to Gideon's troubled spirit.

God knows what we believe, and God knew Gideon believed what Moses said about God applied to angels as well. Therefore, the Bible informs us the Lord Himself spoke to Gideon saying:

"Peace be unto thee; fear not: thou shalt not die" (Judges 6:23).

Gratitude driven, Gideon built an altar and he called it Jehovah-Shalom, meaning "the Lord is Peace." Because there will always be another war, another battle, another struggle, another Al-Qaida, another Taliban, and another Osama bin Laden until Jesus returns, we need a peace the world can't give and the world can't take away.

From the Boston Tea Party to Bunker Hill, there always seems to be another clash. Bosnia, and the beaches of Normandy, Vietnam, Iraq, Desert Storm, Afghanistan, the Gaza Strip, and Gettysburg are all salient reminders we live in a world where there are "wars and rumors of wars" (Mark 13:7).

When Gideon defined God as Jehovah-Shalom, he was not referring to a divine peace that comes after the war is over. He spoke of a blessed possession that can be realized even in the most heated and severe times of battle. Shalom is not simply a picture of a fading and tranquil sunset but that of a small bird resting within a rock as waves from the ocean beat without ceasing. Neither the waters that fell from low-hanging clouds nor the angry winds that blasted the bird's refuge from beneath could keep it from singing a song born out of a peace that creates a safety zone. Jehovah-Shalom—the Lord is our Peace—assures us even though evil will wage war with good, it is a war evil can't win. Shalom does not mean the devil is gone but that the devil is defeated. Jesus told His disciples, "Peace I leave with you, my peace I give unto you. Let not your heart be troubled, neither let it be afraid" (John 14:27).

The peace our Lord gives is not a reward for a life well lived. It is a gift reserved for those who love Him. The peace of God doesn't come from turning over a new leaf, but from receiving a new life. When the disciples found themselves in a storm, they were afraid and rowed desperately. They gave it their best, but their best was not good enough, yet at the darkest hour, Jesus showed up and calmed the wind (Mark 6:47-51).

The Lord could have waved His hand from the beach and the storm would have ceased, but He walked on the water to reach them. The Lord could have spoken a word from the mountaintop and the winds would have ceased to stir, but He walked on the water to comfort them.

In walking on the water to calm the fears of His disciples, the Lord demonstrated an eternal truth about God and spoke a prophetic word of peace to every age. The disciples were worried about the water sinking their boat. Jesus walked on the very thing that made them afraid. By walking on the water, Jesus showed the threat was under His feet. Jesus walked on the very thing that had them shaking in their shoes. Nothing is over His head, even though we see circumstances above our heads. The Lord revealed that whatever is over our heads is already under His Holy feet.

"And the peace of God, which passeth all understanding, shall keep your hearts and minds through Christ Jesus" (Philippians 4:7). Now that's Shalom!

Generally, the view of God's peace in this image is that of a soldier keeping guard, walking his post to protect a place of value. It was to Paul an even more intimate illustration. At this time, Paul was chained to a Roman soldier. He was guarded day and night. Such is the truth of God's abiding watchfulness. When we give our hearts to Christ, God gives to us His peace. This doesn't mean the absence of conflict, but the untiring presence of the One who love us far more than we love ourselves.

The War that Evil Can't Win

"And the servants of the king of Syria said unto him, Their gods are gods of the hills; therefore they were stronger than we; but let us fight against them in the plain, and surely we shall be stronger than they. And there came a man of God, and spake unto the king of Israel, and said, Thus saith the Lord, Because the Syrians have said, The Lord is God of the hills, but he is not God of the valleys, therefore will I deliver all this great multitude into thine hand, and ye shall know that I am the Lord. And they pitched one over against the other seven days. And so it was, that in the seventh day the battle was joined: and the children of Israel slew of the Syrians an hundred thousand footmen in one day. But the rest fled to Aphek, into the city; and there a wall fell upon twenty and seven thousand of the men that were left. And Ben-hadad fled, and came into the city, into an inner chamber. And his servants said unto him, Behold now, we have heard that the kings of the house of Israel are merciful kings: let us, I pray thee, put sackcloth on our loins, and ropes upon our heads, and go out to the king of Israel: peradventure he will save thy life" (1 Kings 20:23, 28-31).

We never reach a state in this world of finishing with those who live like Ben-hadad. Sometimes they work in the places where we work, and sometimes they claim to worship in places where we worship. They are aggressive rather than assertive. They are hard to love and to live with simply because they can be. They might go to church, but they hate everything for which the Church stands.

I was powerfully reminded of this truth late one September day in 1988. I had worked almost to the point of exhaustion to build a program designed for the purpose of lifting up the fragile. I had worked with people no one else wanted to work with. I had hired people no one else would hire. I had labored to make them successful in spite of themselves. I expected gratitude. I received evil. I expected truthfulness, but received a pack of lies. I didn't know at the time I was surrounded by people who had the spirit of an evil Ben-hadad. They didn't achieve and didn't want to learn how to achieve honestly. They only resented my challenge and looked for the best way to blow out my candle so theirs could shine without putting forth the effort that such a prize required.

At the beginning of 1 Kings 20, a Syrian king by the name of Ben-hadad appeared arrogant and invincible. Ben-hadad was an evil-hearted man with immoral plans. He had 32 kings and their resources at his command and seemed to have prepared for several contingencies. He had even mapped out a route for retreat with no real fear of needing to use it. Yet before the chapter concluded, this man became a defeated foe. He dressed in sackcloth, put a rope on his head, and humbled himself to the point of begging for his life from a nation he had humiliated, violated, and totally intimidated.

Empires pregnant with wealth and warriors famous for their feats had all fallen in battle before the might of Ben-hadad. History had been his friend, but when he attacked God's people, he engaged in a war evil couldn't win.

What Adolf Hitler of Germany and Hideki Tojo of Japan couldn't do, a band of terrorists have done by making our homeland into a battlefield. Things are never going to be the same nor should they be the same. We have been reminded in a way that none should ever forget the war we face is one that will not be won quickly or quietly. Outlining our Bibles, analyzing God's attributes, and charting the dates are not enough. Going from seminar to seminar, buying tapes, and studying Greek and Hebrew is not enough. Long before the first terrorist seized the first plane, the beaches of Normandy were invaded on D-Day, before the first drop of blood was shed in the Civil War, Gideon built an altar and called it Jehovah-shalom—the Lord is peace.

During my painful time in 1988, I found this to be true in ways I had not known. The people around me meant it for evil. God used it to promote me to stations beyond my finite imagination. If my false friends had not done what they did, I would not have opened my eyes and my heart to the larger work God had designed for me. With God's grace there is always a brighter day ahead. We must never view the ruins without understanding God has the resources for the reconstruction of the ruins. It is on this assurance the pivot of all history swings from despair to delight. Where sin abounds grace much more abounds. It is this kind of faith that moves mountains and also moves our God to dispense more of His favor.

King Ahab, known more for his wickedness than his goodness, was on the throne as king of Israel when God sent the prophet Elijah to

His people. Elijah's task was to remind God's people God was not dead or deaf, and He had not forsaken the work of His hands. After the prophet spoke, even King Ahab caught a new attitude and replied to Ben-hadad: "Let not him that girdeth on his harness boast himself as he that putteth it off" (1 Kings 20:11).

In today's vernacular Ahab was saying to the overconfident transgressor, "A warrior still dressing for battle should not brag like a warrior who has already won the fight." As far as we know, this is the only wise statement Ahab ever made. Some claim the saying didn't originate with Ahab but was a common proverb during his lifetime. Regardless of the origin, the warning proved true. God's people prevailed, and we can prevail if we can receive the peace God affords before the enemy is down and out for the count. The war is not a war between Christian and Muslim or West against East. It is a war between good and evil, God and the devil, right and wrong, and love and hate. Opportunities are sometimes lost when we are outmaneuvered by clever adversaries. Sometimes we run into people who make promises they can't keep, but in spite of all we face, we serve a God who cannot fail and will not fall.

God's people prevailed because the God of the mountains is God in the valley. The God who brings on the daylight is still God in the thick of the night. He is our Banner, Jehovah-Nissi. He is our Peace. Jehovah-Shalom. Everywhere. Every time. At home or at the hospital. In the cold or in the fire. Through the stress and through the storm. He is our peace.

Dr. Lee Scarborough, an early president of Southwestern Baptist Theological Seminary, once preached a sermon about Jonah being swallowed by a great fish. His young son, who heard the sermon, went home and asked, "Daddy, do you really believe a fish could swallow a man and keep him alive inside of itself for three days and three nights?" The father replied, "Son, if God could make a man out of dust and the first fish out of nothing, don't you think He could make a fish to swallow Jonah?" The small lad looked up and said, "Well, Dad, if you're going to bring God into it that's different." God is the Author of all peace. Bring Him into the battle you fight and the burdens you face. When your heart is aching and the loneliness seems unbearable, bring Him in and experience the difference. Whatever it is you fight or face, remember even if it's over your head, it's always under His feet. I can't bring Him in for you. You must put out the welcome sign and readily invite His residence. His face is already turned your way. He has His sights on you and He's only waiting for you to allow His sight to become your security.

As I recall that difficult time in September 1988, I honestly cannot remember the pain I endured because of the enormous peace the Lord gave me. As a matter of fact, I now rejoice in the peace that kept me while God took what was meant for evil and transformed it into a bounty of blessings. My story is not unique. The peace of God has trophies in every culture, age, and community. For 27 years I have been blessed by God to preach in the Mount Canaan Baptist Church in Talladega, Alabama, each Sunday. I often scan the faces of my parishioners, and I count miracle after miracle of people who know Jesus is our peace. I see it on the faces of widows whose husbands now live in heaven. I see it in the warmth of those who have come out on top, time after time. If you truly bring Him in, you can affirm He is watching over all the affairs of your life and He will make sure your needs are met.

Our God is well-motivated, well-intentioned, and well-equipped. He is the hope that never fades, the strength that never weakens.

You can redefine and rename the people and places designed to defeat you, which the Lord taught David when he defeated the Philistines.

> "But when the Philistines heard that they had anointed David king over Israel, all the Philistines came up to seek David; and David heard of it, and went down to the hold. The Philistines also came and spread themselves in the valley of Rephaim. And David enquired of the Lord, saying, Shall I go up to the Philistines? wilt thou deliver them into mine hand? And the Lord said unto David, Go up: for I will doubtless deliver the Philistines into thine hand. "And David came to Baalperazim,

and David smote them there, and said, The Lord hath broken forth upon mine enemies before me, as the breach of waters. Therefore he called the name of that place Baalperazim. And there they left their images, and David and his men burned them. And the Philistines came up yet again, and spread themselves in the valley of Rephaim. And when David enquired of the Lord, he said, Thou shalt not go up; but fetch a compass behind them, and come upon them over against the mulberry trees. And let it be, when thou hearest the sound of a going in the tops of the mulberry trees, that then thou shalt bestir thyself: for then shall the Lord go out before thee, to smite the host of the Philistines. And David did so, as the Lord had commanded him; and smote the Philistines from Geba until thou come to Gazer" (2 Samuel 5:17-25).

God has a plan and a time in which He employs a process to execute His plan. If you seek His counsel, His peace will enable you to live with hope while you wait with patience for those events you cannot control. Luke 12:37 says, "Blessed are those servants, whom the lord when he cometh shall find watching; verily I say unto you, that he shall gird himself, and make them to sit down to meat, and will come forth and serve them." The word "watching" is translated *gregoreuo* in Greek, which means "to be cautious or give strict attention." The translation implies a sense of hope, of expectation, and of blessed excitement. We watch with a sense of urgency because something great is about to happen and it could happen at any time. We must be ready for Christ's return because no one knows when it will happen. This kind of peace drives away fear by the shining of an inextinguishable ray of hope emanating from the very throne of the eternal God.

The Philistines had received the news that David had become God's anointed over all of Israel. They hated the thought. Be assured when God blesses, the devil always hears about it. The Philistines gathered themselves together in the Valley of Rephaim, which literally means "the valley of the giants." The Philistines mobilized their forces and mapped out their strategy. Even though the Philistines had lost the first battle, they were still a mighty force. The defeat of one evil is never the defeat of all evil. We are in a war whether we feel like it or not. Evil is stubborn and resilient.

David sought God's counsel and was given the green light to attack. The victory came swiftly. The enemy, however, returned after the first defeat. David was too wise to make his daily itinerary according to yesterday's mandate so he sought God anew. Where you worked and warred yesterday might not be your assignment for today, so it's always a good idea to "fall in and get fresh orders" every day. What worked for you in the past might not have any place in your future so don't try to fight today's battles with yesterday's strategies.

When David inquired of the Lord the second time, God gave him a different set of directions. God said:

(1) Don't go up. Don't attack head on like you did the first time.

(2) Circle around behind them close to the mulberry trees.

(3) Don't do anything until you hear a sound like marching feet in the tops of the mulberry trees. This sound will be a signal from God. David obeyed and he struck down the Philistines from Geba to Gazer.

David the valley Baalperazim, which means "the Lord breaks through" or "the place of the breakthrough." The same valley the Philistines considered "the valley of the giants" was renamed by David the "place of the breakthrough."

With God's peace and power you can rename a place as a place of breakthrough that others called your place of breakdown. Whatever name they called you by to hurt you can be discarded and become your breakthrough. What some called your end, you can call your best start. What someone labeled as your downfall can become your ticket to higher ground. Let the world laugh. One day the laugh won't be on you. There are many things I don't understand, but knowing who gets the last laugh is not one of them. David reminds us of this in Psalm 37:13: "The Lord shall laugh at him: for he seeth that his day is coming.'

History records the time when Xerxes, the king of Persia, invaded Greece with an army and navy. The Greek ships were made ready to sail the bay and attack the Persians. Xerxes' sailors roared for a fight, but Themistocles, the Greek commander, delayed. The sailors grew impatient. Discontent almost turned into mutiny, but Themistocles refused to give the orders to advance. Some called him a coward. Others questioned his loyalty, raising suspicions he had sold out to the enemy. Themistocles said nothing. Instead, he waited until the breeze from the land blew. He knew every morning, the breeze from the land blew toward the deep waters. By waiting for the breeze from the land, Themistocles could use the sails to move his ships. The breeze would make it unnecessary for his men to row. Not having to row, every man became a fighter. Delay meant victory and Themistocles proved it clearly.

Wait forwardly. God's breeze will come. You can rename that which was designed to hurt you. The valley of giants is a way of becoming a place of breakthrough for those who have the peace to be patient. When you are fearful of running out of time, put some "and now Lord" on your schedule.

Jehovah-Shalom. Pronounce it, say it, remember it, and live by it daily.

Chapter 4

And Now Lord
Pronounce Him as Jehovah-Rapha

The Lord Who Heals
(Exodus 15:26)

Depict them as you desire. View them as victims. Paint them as preys. Define them as deceived. See them as swindled. Mark them as misinformed. Designate them as duped. Some call them gullible. Some are what the apostle Paul referred to as silly women laden with sins, led away with divers lusts" (2 Timothy 3:6). There are silly men led captive laden with sins, as well.

Some have fallen who can't recall the hour in which they fell. They are living and hurting reminders of our Lord's prophetic words: "For there shall arise false Christs, and false prophets, and shall shew great signs and wonders; insomuch that, if it were possible, they shall deceive the very elect" (Matthew 24:24).

Make no mistake, there is a war being waged in the arena of healing. There are too many casualties. Some have mortgaged their financial future seeking to purchase the healing only God can give. These people fail to comprehend our God is our Father. He is the sanctuary of our defense and the pavilion of our daily protection. He freely gives that which no person can purchase.

There is, in this capricious battle, also a hostile assemblage of those who may be rich and not even know it. The Word of God informs us as His children we have received an inheritance. Romans 8:16-17 says: "The Spirit itself beareth witness with our Spirit, that we are the children of God: And if children, then heirs; heirs of God, and joint-heirs with Christ; if so that we suffer with him, that we may be also glorified together."

The difficulty God has faced in communicating the message of healing has been getting people to believe. When God called Moses to go down and tell the Israelites he had come to deliver them from the hand of Pharaoh, Moses said to God: "Behold, they will not believe me, nor hearken unto my voice: for they will say, The Lord hath not appeared unto thee" (Exodus 4:1).

The Scriptures assure us: "Believe in the Lord your God, so shall ye be established; believe his prophets, so shall ye prosper" (2 Chronicles 20:20).

Unhealed hurt always leads to greater damage. Open wounds afford ideal abodes for infection and corruption. There are many kinds of hurt but there is only one Healer.

"God told the Israelites, If thou wilt diligently hearken to the voice of the Lord thy God, and wilt do that which is right in his sight, and wilt give ear to his commandments, and keep all his statutes, I will put none of these diseases upon thee, which I have brought upon the Egyptians: for I am the Lord that healeth thee" (Exodus 15:26).

Physical pain is no laughing matter. Some never face a day without the unwanted companion of physical pain. Unlike some, I will not promote a "you're still sick because you have no faith" train of thinking. I don't believe it. The Bible doesn't teach it and I refuse to add pages to the Bible or take any pages out of it. Some have misinterpreted the words of almighty God, which were spoken to the Israelites at a specific point in history, as a panacea for freedom from all physical illness for all ages.

God's promise to the Israelite nation was a promise that would keep them free from the diseases that plagued the Egyptians, contingent upon the Israelite's obedience. God never said they wouldn't have headaches, muscle sprains, or other symptoms of physical illness and injury. God never promised us we would live free of cancer, diabetes, and cardiovascular illness, but He promised to heal us. However, He didn't say when, how, or where. He simply said, "I am the Lord that healeth thee" (Exodus 15:26).

Can we be healed because of our faith? There are clear illustrations where we see this truth revealed, including Matthew 9:27-30:

"And when Jesus departed thence, two blind men followed him, crying, and saying, Thou son of David, have mercy on us. And when he was come into the house, the blind men came to him: and Jesus saith unto them, Believe ye that I am able to do this? They said unto him, Yea, Lord. Then he touched their eyes, saying, According to your faith be it unto you. And their eyes were opened; and Jesus straitly charged them, saying, See that no man know it."

There are also clear illustrations where we are introduced to the mystery of the existence of human suffering in the lives of many who experience miracles in mighty ways.

A. God intervened in Isaac's state of fearfulness.

"And Isaac dwelt in Gerar: And the men of the place asked him of his wife; and he said, She is my sister: for he feared to say, She is my wife; lest, said he, the men of the place should kill me for Rebekah; because she was fair to look upon. And it came to pass, when he had been there a long time, that Abimelech king of the Philistines looked out at a window, and saw, and, behold, Isaac was sporting with Rebekah his wife. And Abimelech called Isaac, and said, Behold, of a surety she is thy wife; and how saidst thou, She is my sister? And Isaac said unto him, Because I said, Lest I die for her. And Abimelech said, What is this thou hast done unto us? one of the people might lightly have lien with thy wife, and thou shouldest have brought guiltiness upon us. And Abimelech charged all his people, saying, He that toucheth this man or his wife shall surely be put to death" (Genesis 26:6-11).

B. God mightily blessed the work of Isaac's hands.

"Then Isaac sowed in that land, and received in the same year an hundredfold: and the Lord blessed him. And the man waxed great, and went forward, and grew until he became very great. For he had possession of flocks, and possession of herds, and great store of servants: and the Philistines envied him. For all the wells which his father's servants had digged in the days of Abraham his father, the Philistines had stopped them, and filled them with earth. And Abimelech said unto Isaac, Go from us; for thou art much mightier than we" (Genesis 26:12-16).

C. The same God who often intervened in Isaac's life did not heal him of his vision loss and misguided blessing upon Jacob rather than Esau (Genesis 27:1-40).

God permitted Herod to kill James but delivered Peter. "Now about that time Herod the king stretched forth his hands to vex certain of the church. And he killed James the brother of John with the sword" (Acts 12:1-2).

"And when Herod would have brought him forth, the same night Peter was sleeping between two soldiers, bound with two chains: and the keepers before the door kept the prison. And, behold, the angel of the Lord came upon him, and a light shined in the prison: and he smote Peter on the side, and raised him up, saying Arise up quickly. And his chains fell off from his hands. And the angel said unto him, Gird thyself, and bind on thy sandals. And so he did. And he saith unto him, Cast thy garment about thee, and follow me. And he went out, and followed him; and wist not that it was true which was done by the angel; but thought he saw a vision. When they were past the first and the second ward, they came unto the iron gate that leadeth unto the city; which opened to them of his own accord: and they went out, and passed on through one street; and forthwith the angel departed from him. And when Peter was come to himself, he said, Now I know of a surety, that the Lord hath sent his angel, and hath delivered me out of the hand of Herod, and from all the expectation of the people of the Jews" (Acts 12:6-11).

Why did God save Paul from death in a shipwreck (Acts 27:27-44) but refuse to remove "a thorn in the flesh, the messenger of Satan" (2 Corinthians 12:7)? To me, the only sane answer is God heals according to His will and promotes according to His wisdom. You will never know God's will unless you seek it with an humble faith, making it the priority in your life and not a priority along with others of equal importance. The most important matter in our lives ought to be doing God's will. Never forget a sickbed can become an anointed chariot to glory if it is God's will. A sickbed can become a classroom where you are taught the deeper things of God more effectively than any lesson you'll ever learn jogging along the highway of health. We are not called to measure our strength by ourselves but by God's own omnipotence. If we allow Him, the promises of God will nourish and comfort us with unmeasured healing.

Should you pray for the healing of those who hurt? Of course. Should you pray to stay healthy? Of course you should . . . if you're using your health to glorify God and do His will. Our physical, emotional, relational, and spiritual lives are intertwined. What good does it do to have healthy feet if they are swift to do evil? What value is there in having a healthy heart if it is filled with hate and not love? What worth is there to having 20/20 vision if you never see the face of God in the presence of His goodness? What sanity is there to spend your life making this world a better place only to go to hell because you have not trusted Jesus as your Lord and Savior?

Our healings are often byproducts of seeking first the will of God. As the apostle Paul said, "For this cause I bow my knees unto the Father of our Lord Jesus Christ" (Ephesians 3:14).

God's will for your life is exactly what you would want if you had enough knowledge, wisdom, and resources to bring it to pass for yourself. God's will for you and me is not simply the best, it is the very best. People have different motives for prayer. Some pray out of habit. Don't misunderstand me, prayer as a habit is good, but it should never be done as some routine ritual out of duty. Some pray out of fear and others pray out of greed. They want to be blessed but have no feelings one way or the other for the Blesser. When Paul wrote the Book of

Ephesians he still had his "thorn in the flesh." There is speculation that eyesight had become a problem for Paul, and that was the thorn he to which he was referring.

Although he was lodged in a Roman prison, Paul did not pray about his thorn. God's grace had made it into an instrument that brought about greater service. He didn't pray for better eyesight, for with the useable vision he had left, he had caught a vision of the new heaven. Paul did not pray to be released from prison. Instead, he submitted to God in reverence and prayed for God's will to be done. His first and foremost concern was for the cause of Jesus Christ. The cause for Christ was more important to him than comfort, physical health, or earthly accolades. The cause of Christ had so overwhelmed him it was his greatest passion. Leonardo da Vinci once said, "When once you have tasted flight, you will forever walk the earth with your eyes turned skyward, for there you have been, and there you will always long to return."

The cause of Christ was far more important to him than the most rapturous scenery this planet could afford, and it is the same for all of us who have the eyes to really see it as it is.

Jehovah-Rapha, the Lord who heals, has more than one world in which to work. He has more than one instrument of wellness to employ. And He has far more than our way of defining what healing is. The cause of Christ has made us heirs of all for which others have dreamed, fought, and died. This cause was so much Paul's passion he wrote eloquently and left behind a wisdom for the guidance of future generations.

God takes care of what is His to have us function at our best because this is advantageous to the kingdom of God. If we have the intellect to do maintenance on automobiles and other forms of transportation that serve us best when they are at their best, surely God can be counted on to excel our feeble attempts. Eat a healthy diet and exercise. Do your best to take care of the tent you live in because "your body is the temple of the Holy Ghost" (1 Corinthians 6:19). When you are sick, never fail to seek His healing and claim it by faith using

Isaiah 53:5: "But he was wounded for our transgressions, he was bruised for our iniquities: the chastisement of our peace upon him; and with his stripes we are healed."

Claim the healing you need, but always trust God to heal according to His wisdom. Regardless of our diagnosis, the prognosis is always in His hands. The key to lasting healing, real healing, and needed healing is for the patient to remain in the physician's hands.

The same God who can heal through a surgeon and a pill can do so without either. The God who builds hospitals for the care of the sick can also raise up the sick without medical treatment. Do I believe in divine healing? All healing, if it is real healing, is divine healing. The God who heals does so sometimes naturally and sometimes supernaturally. Pain can crumble before the Word of God. God can make it disappear like the fog on a misty morning gives way to the rising sun.

The blood of Jesus Christ not only justifies but it also redeems. This is the truth Satan hates. The blood of Jesus redeems. In the Bible, Jesus is given many names and titles. He is called Lord, Savior, King, Priest, Mediator, Mighty God, Prince of Peace, and Redeemer. Peter reminded believers of the redeeming power of the blood of Christ when he wrote, "Forasmuch as ye know that ye were not redeemed with corruptible things, as silver and gold, from your vain conversation received by tradition from your fathers; But with the precious blood of Christ, as of a lamb without blemish and without spot" (1 Peter 1:18-19).

During the lifetime of Simon Peter, much of the world was in slavery. Men, women, and children were constantly being marketed. When a person was in bondage as a slave or captive, that person's only hope was to be redeemed. Someone else had to pay for the relief of the captive for they could never get themselves out of the evil system harnessing their lives. Good intentions were not enough, somebody somewhere had to have the resources to redeem them.

In a cathedral in England, there is the effigy of a knight who fought in the Crusades. By his side is the effigy of a lady who loved him. When one scrutinizes the effigy of the lady, it is apparent she has no right hand. Tradition masterfully voices the story of that knight who fought under the leadership of King Richard I, also known as Richard the Lion-Hearted. The knight had been captured. He was held as a prisoner of war. It is said the knight made numerous appeals to Saladin, the sometimes magnanimous Muslim conqueror, to spare his life and set him free for the sake of the love his wife had for him. Saladin scoffed at the knight. He told him that before long his wife would forget him and remarry. The knight, however, assured him his wife would remain faithful to his memory. Saladin asked for proof saying, "If your lady loves you as you say, she will pass my test. I will send a messenger. My messenger will require she cut off her right hand and send it to me in exchange for your freedom." When the lady received the message, she had her right hand severed and sent to Saladin. Upon the receipt of the severed right hand Saladin set the knight free. The severed hand was proof of the lady's devotion to her husband. She redeemed him with the price of her right hand. Jesus Christ redeemed His own, not with silver, gold, or precious stones but with His precious blood.

Regardless of the pains we feel and pills that sometimes don't work, the almighty God has passed the test. Take a good, hard, holy look at the cross. Christ paid the highest cost. That's not only helpful for some of the pains we feel, but also healing for any hurt we experience whether physical, emotional, relational, or spiritual.

The love of Jehovah-Rapha is not theoretical, but a faithful law on which the redeemed can count. There is a world of difference between a theory and a law. While a theory is a proposed explanation, the status is conjectural and debatable; a law is established and accepted.

When Albert Einstein presented his Theory of Relativity to the scientific community, it is said fewer than five scientists in the whole world understood. His formula remained speculation until the atom was split, thus verifying his calculations and establishing his theory as fact. The Bible teaches us God establishes the hearts of people, unblameable in holiness as a result of His love. God is a God of establishment. In the physical world, the criterion separating theory from law is observable and indisputable evidence. In place after place, time after time, God has revealed the fact His work is verifiable. When the serpent's bite was causing death in the wilderness, God healed His people by directing them to look upon a brazen serpent on a pole.

"And the Lord said unto Moses, Make thee a fiery serpent, and set it upon a pole: and it shall come to pass, that every one that is bitten, when he looketh upon it, shall live. And Moses made a serpent of brass, and put it upon a pole, and it came to pass, that if a serpent had bitten any man, when he beheld the serpent of brass, he lived" (Numbers 21:8-9).

It was verifiable. No tricks. No magic. No deception. The only victims recorded were those who refused to look upon what God decreed they look upon. If you can look upon Jesus by faith and receive Him as your Redeemer, you will live. That's verifiable truth.

On Mount Carmel, 450 prophets attempted to advance the theory their god could provide evidence of existence by answering their call by fire. They danced. They made loud noises. They even cut themselves with knives. They engaged in a host of what they called holy actions, but their deeds fell short of being a barometer of spiritual power. Their religion was nothing more than theory. Their prayers, rituals, dancing, cavorting, and incantations were all done in vain (1 Kings 18:16-46).

Then Elijah approached the altar. He dug a trench around the sacrifice and covered it with barrel upon barrel of water until the sacrifice was drenched and the trench was full. Then, without begging, pleading, dancing, or cavorting, Elijah called upon the Lord with a committed heart. God's awesome power was unleashed. Fire fell from the skies. The sacrifice was consumed. The altar and even the stones that lined the altar were turned to dust. On that day the people praised the Lord, for the power of God was established as true by observable, verifiable, and indisputable evidence.

The love of God is also seen in the power of God. Because God is love, love works. It works within us. It worked at the cross when Jesus prayed for His enemies, and it worked in the grave before the angel rolled away the stone. It will work in your life if you can speak the language of God. There is nothing too hard for God. Absolutely nothing. Every test will work for something good. When much is shared, much is learned. The path of the wise is to seek one wiser than himself or herself. It matters not what needs healing the most, always begin the treatment in the Lord Jesus Christ's name and close it with praises to Him. He will do great and wonderful things for you. "Call unto me, and I will answer thee, and shew thee great and mighty things, which thou knowest not" (Jeremiah 33:3).

There is a Senegalese proverb which says, "The opportunity God sends does not wake up him who is asleep." I love the story told about a small rural town that offered a large reward for anyone who had the skills to catch wolves. The wolf population, it seems, grew at a rapid and alarming rate. That reality created a marked decrease in sheep as the wolves feasted at the shepherds' expense. Several shepherds combined their resources and arrived at a sizeable reward designed to motivate others to achieve what they had been unable to terminate. Three brothers, Little Willie, Big Willie, and Willie James, heard about the reward and set out with the goal of making some big money.

They set up their camp, and at nightfall they started a fire and made their beds next to the warm blaze. There was a chill in the night air, but the fire made it comfortable. The serenity of the night made a promise it had no plans to keep; however, all three of them fell asleep under the visible heavens oblivious to any thoughts that sometimes the hunters become the hunted. The thickness of Little Willie's sleep was penetrated by a cold nudge at midnight. He awoke, sat up, and looked around to see the entire campsite surrounded by a group of 52 gleaming wolves' eyes. He pinched himself to make certain he was fully awake and not dreaming. Delighted and enthusiastic, Little Willie grabbed both Big Willie and Willie James. With a big grin on his face he said, "Both of y'all wake up. Man we got bank! Wolves are everywhere! It's time to get paid!"

Now what the wolves may have seen as a midnight snack, Little Willie saw as a bank account and an address on easy street. I don't know about you, but I think it's great when a child of God can think of himself or herself as being rich when surrounded by wolves. The

Bible agrees in James 1:2-4: "My brethren, count it all joy when ye fall into divers temptations; Knowing this, that the trying of your faith worketh patience. But let patience have her perfect work, that ye may be perfect and entire, wanting nothing."

The rule some speak claiming all human sickness will be healed by God in this world, at this time clearly is not true and definitely does not apply to every life that is rich in faith. Reverend Henry Francis Lyte wrote a wonderful hymn in 1847. He suffered with a lung ailment, and his physicians instructed him to relocate from Brixham, England, to the warmer climate of Italy. He had served his congregation in England for 24 years. He was heartbroken, sick, and growing sicker. Out of his illness and need to relocate to a warmer climate, he wrote a prayer. Reverend Lyte never made it to Italy. He died in Nice, France, only two months after leaving England. His prayer became a hymn that has blessed millions of Christians throughout the world. The prayer of a sick minister that became a universal blessing is the hymn "Abide with Me." The first verse says, "Abide with me; fast falls the eventide; The darkness deepens; Lord, with me abide. When other helpers fail and comforts flee, Help of the helpless, O abide with me!"

God promised to heal us; however, He didn't say where, and He didn't say when. Some years ago the Holy Spirit gave me a clear illustration of how God works at times. Our television in the den was in need of repair. I called a repairman. He responded quickly. However, after a while he looked at me and said, "I can repair this television. I know what's wrong. I just can't fix it here. I need to take it to my repair shop. What it needs, I've got, but I need to repair it there before it will work right here."

God knows when we've had enough pain, and there are times when He says no to the church or family who is praying in order to say yes to the ones who are being prayed for. God knows when a soul has outgrown this world. God knows how to get the best from us. Like someone making juice, He simply allows some squeezing to take place in order to get the juice He put in at creation. There is a special kind of music in our souls that only emerges as we are squeezed. Sometimes the most appropriate question we can ask when God maketh us to lie down is not, "When are we going to get out of this?" but rather, "What are we going to give out of this? There are times when God allows us to be placed on a sickbed in order to measure us for greater service.

Sometimes your spirit needs to be healed more than your body. Don't let Satan rob you of this thought, for sometimes a sick body is designed by God to become a cathedral that none can ignore. Without walls there would be no roofs. Without Christians bearing pains as Christians ought to bear pain, the testimony of the saints is reduced to theory. The Lord often makes you lie down in green pastures because He knows there is some spiritual surgery you can't receive while you are on your feet.

A sick spirit is far worse than a sick body. I've seen good people with such sick spirits they infect an entire church. I've seen hurt people with good physical health so sick in spirit they defile and poison their own legacy. Sick spirits create self-righteous breakdowns. Sick spirits in healthy bodies sometimes put revivals on hold and change people we may think we know into people we never thought they could become.

Acts 10 reveals the storied exchange between God and the apostle Peter. A Roman centurion by the name of Cornelius was ripe for entry into the kingdom of God. According to the Bible, Cornelius was:

"A devout man, and one that feared God with all his house, which gave much alms to the people, and prayed to God always" (Acts 10:2).

Cornelius was a treasure. Peter was God's tool to take the treasure. Peter's physical strength had enabled him to travel from Jerusalem to Joppa. There is no hint of any severe bodily injury even though he had suffered a lashing for preaching the Gospel (Acts 5:12-42). The Bible affirms the disciples rejoiced "they were counted worthy to suffer shame for his name" (Acts 5:41b). While Peter's body was fine, his spirit was sick. Peter's spirit was so sick he was too disabled to deal with Cornelius, and God had to rush him into surgery. It happened on Simon the tanner's roof at noon, the sixth hour. Peter was physically hungry. God cut through his physical appetite as he thought about a meal and gave him a vision. In the vision, there were clean and unclean animals. There were those the Jewish diet could endorse wholeheartedly, but there also were "wild beasts and creeping things and fowls of the air" (Acts 10:12). God said "Rise, Peter; kill, and eat" (v. 13). Peter said, "No. I'm hungry, but I have never eaten anything unclean, and I'm not so desperate to do it now." While the wound in his sick spirit was open, God went in. God cut out the racism, the prejudice, and the ingrained evil that made his spirit so sick and prepared him to take the Gospel to the house of Cornelius. When Jehovah-Rapha finished His initial surgery, Peter's post-surgery affirmation was "of a truth I perceive that God is no respecter of persons: But in every nation he that feareth him, and worketh righteousness, is accepted with him" (vv. 34-35).

The Sick Spirit of Judas Killed the Healthy Body of Judas

There is no more vivid illustration of why a distempered, infected, and rabid spirit needs to be healed than in the life of Judas Iscariot.

Regardless of theological arguments and predestination proponents, Judas had some very positive things going for him. Jesus chose him to be one of the original twelve apostles. This was no small honor. Judas accepted Jesus' challenge, which was no minor decision void of cost. Judas additionally impressed the other 11 apostles because they allowed him to carry the bag, which means he was treasurer. Whether he deserved it or not, the 11 other apostles trusted Judas. Examining Judas' life more closely reveals an example of his character.

(1) He watched Mary in order to criticize her. Judas watched the anointment of our Lord prior to His holy death, but he was so sick in his spirit that he criticized rather than rejoiced in what he saw.

> "Then took Mary a pound of ointment of spikenard, very costly, and anointed the feet of Jesus, and wiped his feet with her hair: and the house was filled with the odour of the ointment. Then saith one of his disciples, Judas Iscariot, Simon's son, which should betray him, Why was not this ointment sold for three hundred pence, and given to the poor? This he said, not that he cared for the poor; but because he was a thief, and had the bag,

and bare what was put therein. Then said Jesus, Let her alone: against the day of my burying hath she kept this. For the poor always ye have with you; but me ye have not always" (John 12:3-8).

(2) He watched Jesus in order to receive the sop. Judas took holy communion from the hands of Jesus, but his spirit was so sick he still betrayed Him.

"Jesus answered, He it is, to whom I shall give a sop, when I have dipped it. And when he had dipped the sop, he gave it to Judas Iscariot, the son of Simon. And after the sop Satan entered into him. Then said Jesus unto him, That thou doest, do quickly. Now no man at the table knew for what intent he spake this unto him. For some of them thought, because Judas had the bag, that Jesus had said unto him, Buy those things that we have need of against the feast; or, that he should give something to the poor. He then having received the sop went immediately out: and it was night" (John 13:26-30).

(3) He watched the other 11 apostles in order to deceive them. After Judas' death Peter said, "For he was numbered with us, and had obtained part of this ministry" (Acts 1:17).

Judas had been a student in the school of faith. He had preached the Gospel, healed the sick, cast out demons, received the holy communion from the hand of Jesus, and shared in the evangelism of the cities through which he had passed. Peter said "he had obtained part of this ministry." Judas had watched the stupendous power contention between the forces of good and evil and had done some service and rendered some good on the behalf of the kingdom of God.

(4) He watched the enemies of Jesus in order to bargain with them. Judas could have watched the Lord of glory during His last hours to comfort Him. However, Judas' spirit was so sick the only opportunity he watched for was the opportunity to betray Jesus.

"Then one of the twelve, called Judas Iscariot, went unto the chief priests, and said unto them, What will ye give me, and I will deliver him unto you? And they covenanted with him for thirty pieces of silver. And from that time he sought opportunity to betray him" (Matthew 26:14-16).

(5) Judas watched the floor of the holy place as he cast down his blood money of 30 pieces of silver on it but, he was too sick in his spirit to cast himself down on the mercy of Jehovah-Rapha.

"When the morning was come, all the chief priests and elders of the people took counsel against Jesus to put him to death: And when they had bound him, they led him away, and delivered him to Pontius Pilate the governor. Then Judas, who had betrayed him, when he saw that he was condemned, repented himself, and brought again the thirty pieces of silver to the chief priests and elders, Saying, I have sinned in that I have betrayed the innocent blood. And they said, what is that to us? see thou to that. And he cast down the pieces of silver in the temple, and departed, and went and hanged himself. And the chief priests took the silver pieces, and said, It is not lawful for to put them into the treasury, because it is the price of blood" (Matthew 27:1-6).

The 30 pieces of silver in the hands of a man who loved money to the point he would steal from his friends and sell his Savior symbolized an increased irritability and depression that destroyed him. He had eyes to see, ears to hear, hands to touch, and limbs to move, but his spirit was so sick spiritual fatigue set in and his last physical efforts were used to betray his Savior, the One he claimed to serve. His final fate resulted in a crushing rather than a cleansing. There is a place at the cross for every sin. The sickness of criticism, deception, and covetousness, is a far more dangerous disability than cancer or cardiovascular illness.

Many church people would do good to heed the warning that is obvious. Some people serve their church to the point they feel like nobody else can or should do anything for the church unless the project receives their blessings. Some who are faithful in going and giving are also guilty of condemning and censoring. Some who are the best of the bunch who work in the kitchens should also pray mightily to avoid the sin of setting up a throne and anointing themselves as queens and kings for life. Beware, beloved, because it is often not those who are outside our fold but those who, like Judas, have part in this ministry who do great damage to the kingdom of God. Sometimes the faithful 20 percent who do 80 percent of the work need to get a spiritual checkup to make certain they don't like it that way and are working to keep it that way aggressively and passively. We need the old and the new. We need the young and the old. The old dream great dreams and the young see great visions. The faithful know the way the young have the energy to make the way better. We need seasoned warriors but we also need fresh ideas.

How many ways can we not justify Judas when he said, "save the money for the poor." It was no great disaster that he spoke against Mary as she anointed our Lord. Symptoms of sickness in spirit ought to cause us to rush before Jehovah-Rapha as quickly as we seek Him when we feel a physical pain more intense than any we've known before.

A little cough can become a major problem. A little covetousness in the body of Christ can wreck a strong church unless Christians learn to say "And Now Lord," this church is Your church, this is Your choir, this deacon ministry is Your ministry, this church budget is Your budget. I pronounce you Jehovah-Rapha—you are the Lord who heals.

Little thoughts left to themselves can do great damage. Solomon informs us in the song that bears his name: "It is the little foxes that spoil the vines" (Song of Solomon 2:15). A few years ago a presidential debate with more than one hundred million viewers was held up for 27 minutes. For 27 minutes the president of the United States and the challenger to that office stood silent before a massive television audience. The reason for the 27 minute delay was found in a small gadget that cost less than five dollars. Little problems left to themselves can bring about huge misfortune.

Today, neuroscientists have learned much of what we have thought about the human brain is true. Your brain weighs about sixteen hundred grams, almost three pounds. The brain looks more like a lump of gray cauliflower than a computer, but it functions a lot like a computer. There are three components of a computer, and these three components describe in non-technical language the way in which the brain functions.

(1) The screen is what you use to see what you are programming on your computer. The screen for us is what we reveal to those around us.

(2) The keyboard is what we use to type in directions and information. In our human form, the keyboard is our senses. What we hear, taste, see, touch, smell or anything we say to ourselves. What we tell ourselves we program into our brain. If we are constantly telling ourselves bad stuff it will program the brain with the bad stuff we type into it.

(3) The disk, of course, records the information that you type into it. The disk in a human being is our subconscious mind. What we experience, what we are told, what our ears hear, what our eyes see, what our taste buds taste, what our noses smell, and what our limbs touch are programmed into our brain. Whatever programming we receive is as important and as permanent as any program which has been punched into a computer.

The mental commands which direct and control us are called thoughts. The thoughts you have programmed into your brain, or have allowed others to program into you, are affecting, directing and controlling all you do.

Today, more than ever, countless Christians, churches and causes are being limited and defeated by programs God never intended to take residence in our brains. We are being attacked by Satan through unhealthy thoughts that infect us with racism, classism, denominationalism, and tradition of defiance. We need healing. We need divine healing because of satanic programming.

Satan begins his battle in the arena of our thoughts. He disables the army of the Lord by winning his battle in our thoughts. I have seen churches turn on their fallen. Have you ever thought about the fact that in too many instances the church is the only army that turns on its wounded? When people fall and fail—and they will fall and fail—they need a fellowship that heeds.

"Brethren, if a man be overtaken in a fault, ye which are spiritual, restore such an one in the spirit of meekness; considering thyself, lest thou also be tempted. Bear ye one another's burdens, and so fulfill the law of Christ. For if a man think himself to be something, when he is nothing, he deceiveth himself" (Galatians 6:1-3).

I return to Jehova-Rapha here because often the person who falls needs the loving fellowship of one with whom there has been some problem. Unless the Lord is allowed to heal the hurt of a previous encounter, the one whose fellowship just might be the most treasured and used by God to demonstrate his power will go unused. When we fail and fall we need love and forgiveness from supporters, but we also need love and forgiveness from others in the body of Christ whose condemnation of us is feared. If a friend lifts you when you are down, that's great but when a potential judgment is abated from an adversary that's special. When the one you thought would laugh comes to you with loving tears, something happens in heaven that moves angels to smile and demons to curse. The reason is simple. This kind of reconciliation validates for the world the reality of God's grace and mercy. It demonstrates God's healing power.

When Jacob and Esau met after years of bitterness, self-pity, and anger, I have a feeling their tears were not the only ones falling on the day of their reconciliation.

"And Jacob lifted up his eyes, and looked, and, behold, Esau came, and with him four hundred men. And he divided the children unto Leah, and unto Rachel, and unto the two handmaids. And he put the handmaids and their children foremost, and Leah and her children after, and Rachel and Joseph hindermost. And he passed over before them, and bowed himself to the ground seven times, until he came near to his brother. And Esau ran to meet him; and embraced him, and fell on his neck, and kissed him: and they wept" (Genesis 33:1-4).

The scene speaks for itself. It is saturated with the healing power of the Almighty God. Whoever said time heals all things was wrong. Time alone does not heal all things. Time alone can allow a small infection to become a deadly disease. Time can become an enemy. The treatment of cancer, for instance, is usually most successful when the cancer is detected in its early stages. Prognosis is strongly influenced by the cancer's stage, but it is also affected by one's general state of health. What is true in the physical world is equally true in the spiritual realm.

A symptom is an indication that something is not right in the body. While early symptoms are not easily observed by others, they are often felt or noticed by the sick person. Symptoms such as unexplained weight loss, fever, and fatigue should send the sick body to some place of healing. Symptoms such as sharp criticism of others, envy, and jealousy are symptomatic of the fact that something is wrong in the spiritual body. If left to themselves, these spiritual symptoms will worsen to the point of disaster even in the most church-going of the bunch.

Judas' betrayal of Jesus enlarges the horror of betrayal because he had the privilege of walking, talking, and living with Jesus for three years. Judas, plagued with the sickness of his soul, had the privilege of living with Jesus, yet refused to seek the healing he most needed. Sickness of spirit leads to death of body and soul. Time alone will not change the sad realities where so many of our people are throwing away their lives on drugs, alcohol, and wastefulness in spite of their great privileges. There is a word from our Lord that dramatizes the awesome responsibility that goes with blessed privileges.

"Woe unto thee, Chorazin! Woe unto thee, Bethsaida! For if the mighty works, which were done in you, had been done in Tyre and Sidon, they would have repented long ago in sackcloth and ashes. But I say unto you, it shall be more tolerable for Tyre and Sidon at the day of judgment, than for you. And thou, Capernaum, which art exalted unto heaven, shalt be brought down to hell; for if the mighty works, which have been done in thee, had been done in Sodom, it would have remained until this day. But I say unto you, that it shall be more tolerable for the land of Sodom in the day of judgment than for thee." (Matthew 11:21-24).

Time alone does not result in reconciliation. Time alone can allow a small misunderstanding to become a major entanglement. The same God who heals the body is waiting to heal the spirit that can become so sick it will, like Judas, take Holy Communion from the very hands of Jesus and follow an unholy agenda. David said, "I will set no wicked thing before mine eyes" (Psalm 101:3). He additionally said, "Let the words of my mouth, and the meditation of my heart, be acceptable in thy sight, O Lord" (Psalm 19:14). When we type into our minds the Word of God, it will show up on our screens. The world will see God in us, Christ in us, the Holy Spirit in us, the Word of God in us, love, forgiveness, spiritual power, and amazing physical feats in us.

When Satan types doubts on our keyboard about our salvation, we must retype: "As many as received Him, to them gave He power to become the sons of God, even to them that believe on His name" (John 1:12).

When men say we will never experience a miracle in the healing of our body unless we pay them for it, we must retype: "With His stripes we are healed." (Isaiah 53:5)

When some type into your keyboard that you have a sin that God won't forgive or that you have a condition that God can't overcome you must reprogram, retype into your being the fact that we serve a God who "Forgiveth all our iniquities, and healeth all our diseases" (Psalm 103:3)

"As a man thinkest in his heart, so is he" is forever God's wisdom to every age. We must read good books along with our Bible. We must seek out wise counsel and guard our heads and our hearts with the inerrant, invincible, and inescapable Word of God. During biblical days, a goldsmith often tested and made perfect the gold he worked with by holding it and flooding it in and out of the fire and the water until such time as he could see his face mirrored in the gold. More often, the Almighty God will take us and test us until He sees the face of Jesus as He beholds us. When, in spite of what happens or fails to happen, God looks and sees Jesus in us, then He knows we've been heated in the fire and dipped in the water long enough. When subconsciousness, the disk in us, is programmed with Jesus, the Father knows we have been in the fire and water long enough. Through our tests, trials, and immersions in the fire and flood, the Almighty God convinces those who allow Him that He is Jehovah-Rapha, the Lord who heals.

Jehovah-Rapha—pronounce it, say it, remember it, and live with it. . . . daily.

Chapter 5

And Now Lord
Pronounce Him as:
Jehovah - Tsidkenu

The Lord is our Righteousness
(Jeremiah 23:6)

When you say "and now Lord" pronounce Him as Jehovah-Tsidkenu. Let's just face it: We are all candidates for spiritual failure. The strongest person among us is weak enough to fail. The wisest person among us is foolish enough to sin. This thought is dramatically illustrated in the story of a pastor who accepted his calling to a small church in an inner city. While the church had flourished during it's earlier years, flight to the suburbs resulted in a marked decrease in membership. While prosperous, the church had purchased a parsonage for its pastor, but as the years went by, its treasury could not afford even the purchase of a lawn mower after basic expenses were paid. This was no problem when the pastor arrived in February, but spring arrived, new growth created a lawn in dire need of mowing. One spring morning, the pastor saw a young man pushing a lawn mower down the sidewalk. The pastor approached the young man and asked him if he would like to trade his ten-speed bicycle for his lawn mower. The young man eagerly accepted the trade. After the swap, the young man took off, rode around several blocks, and returned. At his return he saw the pastor standing where he had left him wiping sweat from his weary and wrinkled brow. The pastor called for the young man to come closer and said, "There's something wrong with this mower. I've pulled this rope more than a dozen times and nothing happens. This mower just won't start."

The youth replied, "Pastor, I forgot to tell you. This is a special kind of lawn mower. It will start and it will cut your lawn, but you have to curse it to get it started." The pastor cast a baffled expression toward the youth and said with a tortured voice, "I guess I'm in a whole mess of trouble. I've been a minister for so long I don't think that I can remember how to cuss." The young man with a mischievous grin, retorted, "Oh pastor, just keep pulling on that rope and it'll all come back to you."

We are all at risk of spiritual failure. Conflicting purposes and principles often transform us into walking civil wars. Second Corinthians 4:8 reveals in clear and certain terms our present dilemma:

"We are troubled on every side, yet not distressed; we are perplexed, but not in despair."

The apostle Paul says in Romans 7:15-25, "For that which I do I allow not: for what I would, that do I not; but what I hate, that do I. If then I do that which I would not, I consent unto the law that it is good. Now then it is no more I that do it, but sin that dwelleth in me. For I know that in me (That is, in my flesh), dwelleth no good thing; for to will is present with me; but how to perform that which is good I find not. For the good that I would I do not; but the evil which I would not, that I do. Now if I do that I would not, it is no more I that do it, but sin that dwelleth in me. I find then a law, that, when I would do good, evil is present with me. For I delight in the law of God after the inward man. But I see another law in my members, warring against the law of my mind, that bringing me into captivity to the law of sin which is in my members. O wretched man that I am! Who shall deliver me from the body of this death? I thank God through Jesus Christ our Lord. So then with the mind I myself serve the law of God; but with the flesh the law of sin."

Many New Testament scholars, including two former systematic theology professors from Selma University at Selma, Alabama, the late Drs. Nathan M. Carter and M.C. Cleveland Jr., taught that Paul was probably drawing an analogy from a real life event of his day. While crucifixion was a horrible death it was not the only tool of torture the Romans used. Sometimes when a man committed a murder, he was bound to the corpse. The murderer was literally tied hand-to-hand, limb-to-limb, trunk-to-trunk, head-to-head, and face-to-face to the corpse of his victim. Both were then cast out into the heated desert sun. As death decayed the corpse, it ate into the living man. That man's victim became a body of death for him who was bound to it.

The man could not escape. His only hope for life lay in being delivered. This is our only hope, as well. If you could escape death, maybe you could congratulate yourself, but if you couldn't get the job done and had to be delivered, all praises went to the deliverer.

In the war between good and evil, I rejoice as Paul, saying, "I thank God through Jesus Christ our Lord" for God's deliverance. In the face of every fear, failure, and fright I claim victory because of Jehovah-Tsidkenu. The Lord is my righteousness. When I try to be holy and find out I'm just a saved sinner, I rejoice because He (Jehovah-Tsidkenu) is my righteousness."

Because God is our righteousness, like Noah, we might fall down in the ark, but we'll never, ever, ever, ever fall out of the ark of safety.

Genesis 7:16 says:

"And they that went in, went in male and female of all flesh, as God commanded him; and the Lord shut him in."

This is our security. We have been sealed.

"Now he which stablisheth us with you in Christ, and hath anointed us, is God;/Who hath also sealed us, and given the earnest of the spirit in our hearts" (2 Corinthians 1:21-22).

"That we should be to the praise of his glory, who first trusted in Christ. In whom ye also trusted, after that ye heard the word of truth, the gospel of your salvation; in whom also after that ye believed, ye were sealed with that holy spirit of promise" (Ephesians 1:12-13).

"And grieve not the holy spirit of God, whereby ye are sealed unto the day of redemption" (Ephesians 4:30).

By the grace of God, Noah was shut into the ark of God and his life was spared and all who were with him. We, as Christians, have been sealed through the Lord Jesus Christ in the Lord Jesus Christ. He is the big circle. We are the small dots living, learning, and loving in Him. Nothing touches the dots except that which is permitted to enter the circle. Sometimes we fall down and get pushed down, but we can never be pushed out nor can we ever fall out.

"My sheep hear my voice, and I know them, and they follow me. And I give unto them eternal life; and they shall never perish, neither shall any man pluck them out of my hand. My Father, which gave them me, is greater, than all; and no man is able to pluck them out of my Father's hand" (John 10:27-30).

God alone is our righteousness. God ordains seasons of spiritual growth, and these are often the very reasons why we are shut in. God permits such in order for us to realize the benefits of being sealed.

Liken unto Jonah the disobedient prophet, the nation of Judah was scheduled by the Almighty for a shut in during the days of the prophet Jeremiah. This shut in, unlike Noah's was not for the purpose of rewarding but for the design of reworking.

"And I will gather the remnant of my flock out of all countries whither I have driven them, and will bring them again to their fold; and they shall be fruitful and increase. And I will set up shepherds over them which shall feed them; and they shall fear no more, nor be dismayed, neither shall they be lacking, saith the Lord. Behold the days come, saith the Lord, that I will raise unto David a righteous branch, and a King shall reign and prosper, and shall execute judgment and justice in the earth. In his days Judah shall be saved, and Israel shall dwell safely; and this is his name whereby he shall be called the LORD Our Righteousness" (Jeremiah 23:3-6).

Corrupt leadership led Judah downhill. Following the wrong leadership always reaps, tragic consequences. While leaders must never forget they are held responsible for those entrusted to their care, followers must always remember the wisdom the apostle John wrote:

"Beloved, believe not every spirit, but try the spirits whether they are of God; because many false prophets are gone out into the world. Hereby know ye the spirit of God. Every spirit that confesseth that Jesus Christ is come in the flesh is of God. And every spirit that confesseth not that Jesus Christ is come in the flesh is not of God; and this is that spirit of antichrist, whereof ye have heard that it should come; and even now already is it in the world" (1 John 4:1-3).

Let leaders and followers beware. Leaders are accountable to God for those they influence and lead. Followers, likewise, are accountable to God when they fail to measure leadership by the rod of God's Word. Jeremiah refused to keep silent in the face of oncoming doom and destruction. He contrasted the corrupt leaders of his day with the coming of the Messiah and said, "This is his name whereby he shall be called, the Lord our righteousness." In the face of political strategies that had confused nations, toppled kingdoms, and slain masses, he found a comfort that came from a righteousness that refused not to break or bend to the pressures of passions that could not last because they could not live beyond the times in which they were born.

Silently sitting before God, Jeremiah saw the certainty of disaster and beyond. God, through His righteousness, promised a day of reconciliation. In order to listen one must be silent. Both words have the same letters. L-I-S-T-E-N—S-I-L-E-N-T. When we talk we share, but when we listen we care. Jeremiah cared. His soul sat in silence as the Almighty spoke. Many missed the message. Some ignored the warning, but Jeremiah sat in silence as God spoke.

After having been silent before God, Jeremiah could not be silent before his nation as they broke the speed limits rushing toward their days of doom. As he stood tiptoe to see the outcome, he refused to allow his ears to be deafened by ordinary sounds. With no books to read and no colleagues to drop by, God had spoken, and the speech of God lodged as a voice in his soul that refused not to be heard.

"Then I said, I will not make mention of him, nor speak any more in his name. But his word was in mine heart as a burning fire shut up in my bones, and I was weary with forbearing, and I could not stay" (Jeremiah 20:9).

Silence before God in reverence? Yes. Silence before a people in danger? Never.

In 1938, there was an international conference held in a small French spa town by the name of Evain-Lesbains. The purpose of the conference was to discuss growing evidence of major human rights abuses in Germany. A large number of countries sent delegates. The nation of Germany was not allowed to send a full delegation. However, the Germans did send some observers. These observers were later discovered to be members of the Gestapo. The delegates met all summer during the year of 1938, however, they spent more time in the spa and at famous restaurants than at the task for which they were sent. At the conclusion of their conference, to their everlasting shame and disgrace, that delegation, in spite of clear evidence of major abuses, rendered a sorry report saying "matters were confined to German internal affairs." They did not call for any changes. The Germans sent observers because their government feared world opinion at that time. According to documents obtained after the war, it was obvious, had the delegates at the conference condemned the evil practices at that time, many of them would have been stopped. If the delegates had only spoken out, many of the concentration camps might never have been turned into death camps. If they had only spoken out, thousands, maybe millions, might have been spared.

In the face of dangerous rumors and real wars, "The Lord is our righteousness." Bad things happen to good people. Unfair things happen to righteous people. Unjust things happen to special, wonderful, and loving people whose minds are keen and hearts are clean. In spite of it all, the Lord is our righteousness. Jesus did not come into this world to give us explanations. He came to give us something sweeter, something better, something far more valuable. He came to be what we are in order to make us into what He is. He is our righteousness when demons accuse us—and they will—when enemies attack us—and they will—and when the spirit is willing and the flesh is weak—and it will be. "Cast all your care upon Him; for He cares for you" (1 Peter 5:7).

No failure is final; no guilt has to be eternal. You will fall. Don't forget, when you fall, nothing of God fails. When you win some and lose some, remember God never loses; He is our righteousness. Say goodbye to guilt. Down? Maybe, but you don't have to be out. Look up. Look out. Say, "and now Lord," You are Jehovah-Tsidkenu.

On December 22, 1989, God gave the world a sign He is the Righteous One and He always comes out a winner at the finishing line. Stalin had built a fortress from the Baltic to the Adriatic Sea. It held some 100 million human souls. After years of solid power the hard-line Romanian Regime fell. It fell just as the walls of Jericho fell, and it fell for the same reason the walls of Jericho fell. It fell because God alone is sovereign and righteous. God alone "rules the nations." God alone says, "Behold all souls are Mine, the soul of the Father, as well as the soul of the son, is mine."

Righteousness will prevail. You can share the victory. If you are having trouble and you have put them on the altar, be of good cheer. "Trouble don't last always," but righteousness does. If you are going through brokenness and you have given it to God, be of good cheer. Righteousness will restore what needs to be restored. Take comfort. Take time to hide and take time to heal. "And now LORD," You are Jehovah-Tsidkenu.

When God is your righteousness, suicide should have no place in your future. In the war between good and evil, we have lost far too many soldiers to death by suicide. I am keenly aware of the fact this is a subject we seek to avoid in our teaching, preaching, and reaching. While it is obvious this is a discussion long overdue, it is also a topic we seek to avoid. It is a problem we keep in the background until it happens, and when it occurs misinformation, shame, incompetence, and awkwardness rules. It is evaded, shunned, and kept at arm's length until we are forced to face it when it claims the life of someone we value, whether it be a family member or a celebrity. Driven to deal with it, we do what we must and try as quickly as possible to place it in the past.

How many times have we heard or even asked the question ourselves, "If a person commits suicide can he or she be forgiven?" How many times have we listened as someone quotes the questions. "The Bible says, "Thou shalt not kill, so if a person kills himself or herself how can he or she go to heaven?"

Extremely uncomfortable in saying anything negative about the deceased in public, we paint the best face we can upon the matter and move onto less taxing themes. The problem with our historical approach to this matter is the rising numbers affected by this taboo subject in communities across our nation. We have been facing a growing phenomenon in America since the late 1970s. This phenomenon well may prove to be a bellwether for our entire culture as we take notice of the alarming rate of suicides among young African Americans. According to the Center for Disease Control and Prevention, suicide is now the third leading cause of death behind homicides and accidents for African Americans between the ages of 15 and 24. Often what we label as drug overdoses are deaths by suicide. In April of 1999, two young, white male students killed fifteen people at a high school in Littleton, Colorado. They also committed suicide.

In 1999, the Surgeon General of the United States released a report addressing the matter of suicide in our country. While he offered a long list of risk factors pointing to mental illnesses, such as bipolar disorder, family history of suicide, alcohol and substance abuse, he also pointed out a list of risk factors such as:

    Hopelessness

    Physical illness

    Cultural and religious beliefs

    Isolation

Suicide as a contagious influence

Let's consider the kind of God we serve. God is love, and because God is love nobody asks, "If a person dies from skin cancer will he or she go to heaven?" Nobody asks, "If a young man dies of Hodgkin's Disease does it mean his soul is lost?" Nobody raises questions about these deaths because they are recognized as diseases. Mental illnesses that might result in suicide are diseases as much as Leukemia is a disease. God, even in our most basic understanding, is too good, too merciful, and too kind to close the gates of glory to one who dies of a disease. Suicide, in cases of mental illness, is surely as covered by the righteousness of God as a baby is covered by the grace of God or a child is covered before the child reaches the age of accountability. Mental illness caused by a chemical imbalance is a disease. God never holds us responsible for anything for which we are incapable of being responsible. As Christians, we must leave to God that which only God can comprehend, and we must help the mentally ill receive treatment as much as we would help anyone stricken with another disease. Mental illness is no illness to elicit shame. William Cowper was institutionalized four times for mental illness. He tried to commit suicide by drowning and by poisoning himself. He also tried to hang himself with a garter but the garter broke. Before he died at age 69 on April 25, 1800, he wrote the hymn:

"Oh, for a closer walk with God,

A calm and heavenly frame,

A light to shine upon the road

That leads me to the Lamb."

God works through people to reach people. With treatment, the mentally ill can live useful lives that bless all of us. God is our righteousness. We must allow the righteousness of God to remove any stigma or shame felt by those who have nothing to be ashamed of because of their illness. God has work that can be done by the mentally ill, and suicide meets its match in God's righteousness.

Four who committed suicide in the Bible due to hopelessness were:

(1) King Saul, the first king of Israel. "Then said Saul unto his armour-bearer, draw thy sword, and thrust me through therewith; lest these uncircumcised come and thrust me through, and abuse me. But his armour-bearer would not, for he was sore afraid. Therefore Saul took a sword and fell upon it" (1 Samuel 31:4).

(2) Saul's armour bearer. "And when his armour-bearer saw that Saul was dead, he fell likewise upon his sword, and died with him" (1 Samuel 31:5).

(3) Ahithophel, the grandfather of Bathsheba. "And when Ahithophel saw that his counsel was not followed, he saddled his ass, and arose, and got him home to his house, to his city, and put his household in order, and hanged himself, and died, and was buried in the sepulcher of his father" (2 Samuel 17:23).

(4) Judas Iscariot, the man who betrayed Jesus. "And he cast down the pieces of silver in the temple and departed and went and hanged himself" (Matthew 27:5).

Hopelessness is the common thread that led to these four men who committed suicide. Saul was a man who had a great looking exterior, but his interior was shabby. He was Israel's first king. He stood "head and shoulders" above others. He was a tall man physically, but he was a small man in God's sight. His ongoing rebellion led him to such a state of hopelessness that he took his own sword and fell on it. He didn't look to God. He followed the theme of his life and took matters into his own hands.

The Surgeon General's call to action to prevent suicide listed one risk factor as local epidemics of suicide that have a contagious influence. This we see clearly revealed as King Saul's young armour bearer followed his example of suicide. The young man had the wherewithal to resist the king's order to slay him but at Saul's suicide he lost hope for the future. A sense of failure gripped his heart and he didn't pray. He, like King Saul, took matters into his own hands.

Ahithophel hated David. He joined Absolom, David's rebellious son. David responded in 2 Samuel 15:31, which reads,

"And one told David saying Ahithophel is among the conspirators with Absalom. And David said, O Lord, I pray thee, turn the counsel of Ahithophel into foolishness."

The Bible informs us God answered David's prayer at 2 Samuel 17:14, which reads: "And Absalom and all the men of Israel said, the counsel of Hushai the Archite is better than the counsel of Ahithophel. For the Lord had appointed to defeat the good counsel of Ahithophel, to the intent the Lord might bring evil upon Absalom."

Faced with rejection and failure Ahithophel did not turn to God in sorrow. He, like Saul and Saul's armour bearer, took matters into his own hands, set his house in order, and committed suicide by hanging himself. He saw no way to recover from the choices he had made, so he added one final choice to a list that never included seeking Jehova-Tsidkenu.

Judas Iscariot saw no way out. His conscience attacked him. The Bible says in Numbers 32:23: "Ye have sinned against the Lord:/and be sure your sin will find you out."

All sin of any kind hurts and degrades and needs to be forgiven. It does not simply do things to us; it does things in us. Our righteousness will fail. We all will sin. Unforgiven sin has the invisible and mysterious kingdom of conscience in which to work and to war. Literature is filled with a host of illustrations.

In *Macbeth,* Shakespeare presents Macbeth immediately after he has murdered the king in order to fuel his ambitions. He speaks to his wife saying he heard the watchman say, "God bless us." He says he tried to say "amen," but the word stuck in his throat. Feeling the pangs of an offended conscience, he realized God is righteous and therefore not on his side. He tries but cannot say "amen" due to a guilty conscience.

In *Lady Macbeth,* Shakespeare goes further and reveals the impossible task of erasing the memory of an evil deed. With firmness Lady Macbeth had driven her husband's determination to murder the king who was his own cousin, in order to reign on the throne of Scotland.

After the plans were carried out and the king was found stabbed to death, they raised the loudest lamentations, and Macbeth was seated on the throne he so coveted.

Things were not perfect, however. People were suspicious. More killings were required. More blood had to be shed. After the king's death, Macbeth looked at his hands. They appeared bloody. His wife instructed him to simply use a little water and the blood would be washed away. As time passed however, Lady Macbeth's conscience began to bite. She worked hard to be composed during the day, but at night she began to walk in her sleep. She struggled with her guilty memories until her mind snapped and she who was so strong died a tortured death, possibly by her own hands.

Those lessons teach the overpowering impact of an accusing conscience. The Bible says, "The wicked fleeth and no man chases." People might not know what you have done, but you know, and you can't outrun yourself. The only hope we have is "the Lord of our righteousness." He alone is able to cleanse us and create in us a clean heart as He renews within us a right spirit. This is our hope, and it is a present help in the times of trouble.

Confronted with the evil he had done, Judas, like the other three men, Saul, Saul's armour bearer, and Ahithophel, took matters into their own hands and committed suicide. It was not the answer then, and it is not the answer now. The only answer, the best answer, God's answer, is found in the prayer of our Lord as He prayed in the Garden of Gethsemane. The cup before our Lord included repeated sins (sins you promised never to commit again), bitter dregs, and all forms of sin, all kinds of failures, all kinds of mistakes, and every vile thing humankind could commit. Jesus drained the cup dry. He died so you would not have to. He bore the cross so you and I could say to those who accuse us, "the Lord is our Righteousness." He can clean up what you messed up. He can give you back what you thought was lost forever. We need you in the army. When you fail—and you will fail—don't take matters into your hands. Look to Him and say, "And now, Lord, I am in Your hands. You are my Righteousness. Forgive me and teach me how to forgive myself. I have made my aim that which in the end will turn out to be my poison if left to myself. Slow though my dying be, I am headed for dated suicide if I lean on my righteousness alone. I thank Thee. I don't have to die. I thank Thee that I can live, and the rest of my life can become the best of my life. I bless Thee that thou art Jehovah-Tsidkenu."

Pronounce it, say it, remember it, and live with it daily.

Chapter 6

AND NOW LORD
Pronounce Him as:
Jehovah-Shammah

The Lord is Present

"It was round about eighteen thousand measures: and the name of the city from that day shall be, The Lord is there" (Ezekiel 48:35, KJV).

Some time ago I viewed a cartoon depicting a school where a student had used a handgun to shoot several other students. In the wake of the disaster one student asked another, "How could God let something like this happen?" The student being questioned replied, "God couldn't do anything to stop it because He is not allowed on the school campus." While I understand the message, I can't help but question the theology. No one should ever see the God of the Bible as being unable to do anything because He is not allowed to be present. This fallacy has a tendency to make people feel safe only in certain places. The God of the church is God beyond the church. The God of the communion table is also God wherever the rubber meets the road. God's presence is never at the mercy of a school board vote or a formal invocation before a football game.

    A.   God is too big to lock up.

"But will God indeed dwell on the earth? behold, the heaven and heaven of heavens cannot contain thee; how much less this house that I have builded?" (1 Kings 8:27, KJV).

B.   God is too strong to lock out.

"Belshazzar the king made a great feast to a thousand of his lords, and drank wine before the thousand. Belshazzar, whiles he tasted the wine, commanded to bring the golden and silver vessels which his father Nebuchadnezzar had taken out of the temple which was in Jerusalem; that the king, and his princes, his wives, and his concubines, might drink therein. Then they brought the golden vessels that were taken out of the temple of the house of God which was at Jerusalem; and the king, and his princes, his wives, and his concubines, drank in them. They drank wine, and praised the gods of gold, and of silver, of brass, of iron, of wood, and of stone. In the same hour came forth fingers of man's hand, and wrote over against the candlestick upon the plaster of the wall of the king's palace: and the king saw the part of the hand that wrote. Then the king's countenance was changed, and his thoughts troubled him, so that the joints of his loins were loosed, and his knees smote one against another" (Daniel 5:1-6, KJV).

Sixty-six years after Nebuchadnezzar's victory over Jerusalem his grandson Belshazzar co-reigned with his father Nabonidus over the Babylonians. Nabonidus spent most of his time away from the kingdom on foreign expeditions while Belshazzar remained in the city of Babylon. God says in Isaiah 46:9-10: "Remember the former things of old: for I am God, and there is none else; I am God, and there is none like me. Declaring the end from the beginning, and from ancient times the things that are not yet done, saying, My counsel shall stand, and I will do all my pleasure" (KJV).

Long before the first Babylonian soldiers set foot on the soil of Jerusalem, Jeremiah spoke to the nation saying God had declared: "And now have I given all these lands into the hand of Nebuchadnezzar the king of Babylon, my servant; and the beasts of the field have I given him also to serve him. And all nation shall serve him, and his son, and his son's son, until the very time of his land come; and then many nations and great kings shall serve themselves of him."

Clearly from these words, the kingdom of Babylon was foretold to last through the life of a son and a grandson of King Nebuchadnezzar. When Belshazzar offered a position in the kingdom to Daniel for interpreting the handwriting on the wall, it was not to be the second ruler but the third ruler in the vast kingdom. Nabonidus was the first ruler and Belshazzar was second to his father. As third ruler, Daniel would be behind Belshazzar.

If anybody could have locked God out it was Belshazzar. His father was away, possibly trying to reopen trade routes, and Belshazzar was in charge of the kingdom that had appeared unto Nebuchadnezzar as a head of gold. Belshazzar threw a party and invited 1,000 of his lords. He insulted the Almighty God as he, his princes, his wives, and his concubines drank wine from golden vessels that were taken out of the temple of God, which was at Jerusalem.

While he was feasting, the providence of God rolled on. Gobnyas, the median general in charge at that time, was besieging the city of Babylon. While Belshazzar was offending God, there was no sound of thunder and no sight of lightning. There were no plagues of frogs or swarms of flies and no rivers were turned into blood. The providence of God rolled on. No seas opened up, but the Medes detoured the Euphrates River back into it's channel, and the army that could not go over the walls, which were three hundred feet high and wide enough for four chariots to travel side by side, went under the walls that protected the city that some had called impregnable.

The Bible says in Daniel 5 that without being toasted and without an invitation, God revealed His presence in the form of a hand. That hand wrote a message of judgment from a God who knew what was going on. God did not frustrate the gold and silver Belshazzar had in store, and he might not frustrate the money you and I might have in the bank, but He knows what is going on.

"Whither shall I go from thy spirit? Or whither shall I flee from thy presence? If I ascend up into heaven, thou art there: if I make my bed in hell, behold, thou art there. If I take the wings of the morning, and dwell in the uttermost parts of the sea. Even there shall thy hand lead me, and thy right hand shall hold me. If I say, surely the darkness shall cover me; even the night shall be light about me. Yea, the darkness hideth not from thee; but the night shineth as the day: the darkness and the light are both alike to thee."

Neither distance nor darkness can hide anything or anyone from God. Some of us might have more sand on the bottom of our hourglass than at the top. Regardless of time and tide God knows our hearts and He orders our steps.

"Neither is there any creature that is not manifest in his sight: but all things are naked and opened unto the eyes of him with whom we have to do" (Hebrews 4:13, KJV).

God's presence as Creator is not the same as Protector and Provider.

The last verse of the last chapter of the book of Ezekiel speaks of a new name for the city of Jerusalem. The new Jerusalem will be given the new name of Jehovah-Shammah—"The Lord is There "or" The Lord is Present." God had been present as Creator when the mighty Babylonian army overthrew the city, but His protective presence had been withdrawn because the people refused to repent of their sins. God had been patient, but divine patience is not divine permission. Ezekiel served his people for 22 years while they were captives in Babylon. During his ministry, God instructed him to illustrate his sermons by role play and role rehearsal. Some of the roles he used included lying part of the day of each day for 390 days on his left side and 40 days on his right side. During this time, the only food he could eat was one eighth ounce meal each day that was cooked over manure. Ezekiel was also commanded by God to shave his head and beard. Lying bound for the 390-day intervals symbolized the many years Israel and Judah had sinned. The shaving of the hair represented the inhabitants of Jerusalem who would face famine, sword, and captivity due to the absence of God's protection.

God is present everywhere as Creator, but He is not present everywhere as Protector and Provider. This is not only an Old Testament concept. On the Monday morning following Palm Sunday, Jesus traveled the road from Bethany to Jerusalem. A fruitless fig tree caught His attention (Mark 11:12-24). He who made the fig tree cursed it, and the next Tuesday morning Peter said, "Master, behold, the fig tree which thou cursedst is withered away." The Christ who came to save showed up as the God who refused to tolerate uselessness. Jesus was present on that dusty Monday morning road but His protection was gone from that tree. Let none be deceived: When God's protection is gone, there is nothing left that can protect.

God doesn't have to send locusts, rain down fire, or make the earth quake to "pay the wages of sin." The only thing God has to do to make certain sin is punished is withdraw His protective presence and the flesh, the world, or the devil will get the job done. Flesh and blood cannot inherit the kingdom of God. The world loves darkness rather than light, and the devil goes forth as a roaring lion seeking someone to devour.

Unforgiven Sin and Unforgiven Sinners

The worst sin of all is the sin that has not been forgiven. The worst sinner of all sinners is the one who has not been forgiven through the blood of Jesus Christ of all his or her sins. Unforgiven sins and unrepentant sinners force either God's protective departure or the deadly destruction from God due to His holiness. God is love, but His love is holy love. God is patient, but His patience is holy patience. In His mercy, sometimes God will depart from a person, a people, or a place in order to avoid their total destruction. There is nothing the flesh, the world, or the devil can do that God can't undo if God is given a chance before time runs out. There is no sorrow He can't heal, no stain He can't clean, and no repentant sinner He can't redeem if the sinner repents before time runs out. While it is dangerous to try and live without God's presence, it is just as dangerous to try and live in His presence with unforgiven sin. Rebellion will reap the removal of real protection and lasting provision.

In my prayer life, I repent daily. I seek God's forgiveness for all of my sins, which include shallow faith at times, omission of all the good I should do, and commission of the things I should never do or think but have done and thought. The light switched on for me the day I learned God's holiness does not grade on the curve. When Jesus and not other Christians became my standard to reach, I became a man who repents daily. The question that humbles me is not the question of whether I love people; I know I do. The question that keeps me humble is, "Do I love people as Jesus loves them?" The question for me is not one of whether I can forgive others; I know in my heart that I have. The question that breaks my heart is have I forgiven others as Jesus has forgiven them and as He has forgiven me. I want many things, but more important than anything else, I want to be holy. I want to be holy like my heavenly Father. I want to be holy like my Jesus, and when I consider His holiness and my feeble attempts, I marvel that He loves me at all. The question for me is not a question of whether I am patient. I recall scores of blessings that have come by my patience. The question is, "Am I as patient as Jesus, and is my patience a holy patience like the holy patience of the God, whom I love far more than I love my life?"

I know what results from a contrite heart bowing before the Almighty. I have experienced the power of holy anointments after coming out of the presence of God before standing in the midst of needy people. I have read physician's reports and studied surgeon's assessments. I have listened as medical specialists have proclaimed "the end has come" for some of my parishioners, but who are still living years beyond the date they were supposed to die. I know what it is like to face a frightened family with nothing but the Word of God. I can tell you that when you, in a repentant spirit and contrite heart, reach the point where all you have is God, you will find out God is enough. I know what it is to be confronted with the presence of demonic forces, and I also know what it is like to bind them in the name of Jesus. Such holy power always evades the arrogant. God refuses to trust this kind of holy favor to the proud and boastful. There is a chasm between God and the unrepentant.

"Thou art of purer eyes than to behold evil, and canst not look on iniquity: wherefore lookest thou upon them that deal treacherously, and holdest thy tongue when the wicked devoureth the man that is more righteous than he?" (Habakkuk 1:13).

God's Wilderness Proposal

"And the Lord said unto Moses, Depart, and go up hence, thou and the people which thou hast brought up out of the land of Egypt, unto the land which I sware unto Abraham, to Isaac, and to Jacob, saying, Unto thy seed will I give it: And I will send an angel before thee; and I will drive out the Canaanite, the Amorite, and the Hittite, and the Perizzite, the Hivite, and the Jebusite: Unto a land flowing with milk and honey: for I will not go up in the midst of thee; for thou art a stiffnecked people: lest I consume thee in the way. And when the people heard these evil tidings, they mourned: and no man did put on him his ornaments. For the Lord had said unto Moses, Say unto the children of Israel, Ye are a stiffnecked people: I will come up into the midst of thee in a moment, and consume thee: therefore now put off thy ornaments from thee, that I may know what to do unto thee" (Exodus 33:1-5).

God's wilderness proposal to Moses reveals the certainty of destruction of the unrepentant and the price Moses was willing to pay to avoid that destruction by his withdrawal. Our heavenly Father's desire to be with His children is so intense it is beyond our ability to comprehend. The God who refuses to forsake the redeemed for one moment is willing to deprive Himself of the apple of his eye in order to avert their deserved destruction. In other words, there are times when God withdraws His protective presence and watches our punishment from sin rather than passing the judgment we deserve. Christians need many things, but there is no need greater than our need to walk humbly before God with a repentant spirit. An unrepentant heart in a Christian's life will not result in the loss of salvation, but will conclude with a loss of holy power. It will not cost you heaven, but it will cost you the holiness you need in order to have daily fellowship with God. When the Lord commanded the people to "put off" their ornaments He was requiring them to repent. The ornaments they wore were symbols they had used in idol worship. God cannot dwell with unrepentant sinners. He must either depart from them or destroy them. Don't miss the lesson of Exodus 33:6: "And the children of Israel stripped themselves of their ornaments by the mount Horeb."

Moses interceded for the people, but his plea would have fallen on deaf ears if the people had not repented and stripped themselves of the ornaments that offended the true and living God. There are some things that cannot be substituted for. Rotating your car tires will not take the place of changing your car's oil. Brushing your hair will not take the place of brushing your teeth. Washing your windows won't take the place of washing your clothes. Saying your prayers won't take the place of praying your prayers. God consented to let His presence go with the nation, but the formula for success not only included Moses' plea, but the people "putting off" their offensive ornaments.

The Difference that Makes the Difference

The theme of the presence of God winning victories runs throughout the Bible. It runs through the Bible because it runs through life.

"By faith they passed through the Red sea as by dry land: which the Egyptians assaying to do were drowned" (Hebrews 11:29).

For the Israelites, the Red Sea event was a jubilee, but for the Egyptians it was a judgment. Both groups arrived at the same barrier, but for the people whose faith made it possible for God to be present with them, the barrier became a blessing. For the other group, the barrier became a burial. One found life; the other found death. God doesn't travel to "Red Seas" with His protective and provisional presence with people who have no faith in Him.

"But without faith it is impossible to please him: for he that cometh to God must believe that he is, and that he is a rewarder of them that diligently seek him" (Hebrews 11:6, KJV).

When "Red Seas" confront you, you'd better be sure you have the resource to cross over, or you will become food for some fish. When storms come you can stand if you've fastened yourself to a foundation the storm can't move. "Red Seas" care nothing for your resumè, and they flow on totally oblivious to pedigrees. "Red Seas" are totally unimpressed with your ability to swim, sail, or sink. "Red Seas" obey only one force, and that force is the Almighty Word of the Almighty God. You might skip over streams on your own. You might run through shallow waters in your own strength, but "Red Seas" are too wide to swim and too deep to take lightly. "Red Seas" do not discern the difference between muscles and measles. When pharaoh arrived at the Red Sea, he arrived without God's protection and he paid the price (Exodus 14:22-31).

"Red Seas" confront us all. They come in different forms. For some it is a disease that killed a strong loved one, and we are afraid that because it took her or him it will claim us, as well. For others it could be a marriage falling apart or a pink slip from a job they thought they could retire from. A painful loss or a public shame, "Red Seas" are big obstacles, but our God provides for us as the years go by and the frost of age falls upon our heads. "Red Seas" come and go, but He abides.

A Symbol of His Presence

God's *fatherly* presence empowers us to wait for His active hand, even when it seems all things are against us. No person lives so alone as the one without the abiding fellowship of God's loving presence. It is that presence of God, recognized or unrecognized, that multiplies the good and divides the bad.

Troubled, fearful, and geographically unconnected to family, Jacob arrived at a place called Bethel. Bethel was a barren landscape that appeared to afford no place for divine visitation, let alone divine residence. Yet, Jacob confessed, "Surely the Lord is in this place; and I knew it not" (Genesis 28:16). Recognized or unrecognized, it is God's *fatherly* presence that allows us to experience dream sleep even when our dreams appear to be out of reach. "It is vain for you to rise up early, to sit up late, to eat the bread of sorrows: for so he giveth his beloved sleep" (Psalm 127:2).

After a day's journey through the wilderness the prophet Elijah sat under a juniper tree. The Bible informs us "he requested for himself that he might die; and said, It is enough; now, O Lord, take away my life; for I am not better than my fathers" (1 Kings 19:4). God did not answer Elijah's request, as a matter of fact, it appears God totally ignored it and put him to sleep before any voice from heaven spoke to him. Shocked by the indefatigability of evil, Elijah made the mistake of taking himself too seriously while failing to take God seriously enough. Doubt, disappointment, despair, and spiritual malaise stole his strength. God didn't listen to his prayer, but he did meet his deepest need by first putting him to sleep.

"The innocent sleep

Sleep that binds up the raveled sleeve of care,

Balm of hurt minds, great

Nature's second course,

Chief nourisher in life's feast"

(*Macbeth*, act II, sc. II).

It was through his sleep that God provided Elijah with insight, rest, and inspiration. Through his sleep, "the chief nourisher of life's feast," who is God, renewed Elijah's spirit and mind so his outlook would match the facts that confronted him. Elijah had no need to fear the future or doubt the outcome, so God put him to sleep so he would be able to internalize heaven's mathematics. When Elijah counted God's supporters in the land, he counted one, which was himself. However, when God counted, God said:

"Yet I have left me seven thousand in Israel, all the knees which have not bowed unto Baal, and every mouth which hath not kissed him" (I Kings 19:18).

Sometimes the most spiritual thing you can do for yourself is to take a nap and rest for a while. When fatigue stands up, sometimes faith sits down and the most spiritual task you can embrace is to slow down until you can stop and allow the Lord to recharge, repair, and renew you. No matter how much God blesses us, He will never bless us with so much we will not need Him every day of our lives.

There is a River

"Though the waters thereof roar and be troubled, though the mountains shake with the swelling thereof. Selah. There is a river, the streams whereof shall make glad the city of God, the holy place of the tabernacles of the most High. God is in the midst of her; she shall not be moved: God shall help her, and that right early. The heathen raged, the kingdoms were moved: he uttered his voice, the earth melted. The Lord of hosts is with us; the God of Jacob is our refuge. Selah" (Psalm 46:3-7). God will not change regardless of the chances and changes that confront our lives. The Psalmist of Psalm 46 saw a consistent, unending, and unstoppable river flowing through the city of God even when alien armies besieged it.

The best time to prepare for a storm is before the winds begin to blow. Long before the Assyrian army surrounded the city of Jerusalem, King Hezekiah ensured the city would have an unending source of water. He diverted the spring of Gihon that was located in the Kidron Valley, located east of Jerusalem. He diverted the water source through a conduit cut out of solid rock into a reservoir within the walls of the city. He then had the conduit covered so the enemy troops could pitch their tents over it and never know hidden in the ground beneath their feet was "a river," "a stream," a water source that "made glad the city of God" (verse 4). The enemy was strong. The troops of opposition were many, but God's people had a pipeline of fresh water that kept them from thirst and tragedy, and the enemy didn't see it.

This conduit, almost *2,000* feet long, flowed unseen beneath the feet of those who sought to destroy the people of God. This is, of course, a prophetical portrait of the life-giving work of our Lord and Savior Jesus Christ. Some who are waiting for us to fall have been waiting for a long time. Their prophecies of doom have proven false time after time. They don't see the source of our strength. As a matter of fact, everything made visible to their eyes suggest our demise and our defeat. Yet, by God's grace, we not only survive—we thrive. We become, by God's grace, a mysterious people to the carnal mind. The evidence that can be seen, touched, heard, felt, and smelled say we should have been "dead and gone" a long time ago. Instead, we, like the Energizer Bunny, keep going, and going, and going. We keep going from miracle to miracle. We keep going from deliverance to deliverance. We keep going from blessing to blessing. We keep going from victory to victory, and the fact we keep going proves Satan is a liar and God is not *some* powerful but is *all* powerful.

Jesus Christ is our unfailing Source of inner refreshment. He is the Reservoir of spiritual water. He comes and He leaves according to His holy desire. He renews according to His inclination, and nobody can stop Him. He flows when and where He pleases.

"The woman saith unto him, Sir, thou hast nothing to draw with, and the well is deep: from whence then hast thou that living water: Art thou greater than our father Jacob, which gave us the well, and drank thereof himself, and his children, and his cattle: Jesus answered and said unto her, Whosoever drinketh of this water shall thirst again: But whosoever drinketh of the water that I shall give him shall never thirst; but the water that I shall give him shall be in him a well of water springing up into everlasting life"(John 4:11-14).

"In the last day, that great day of the feast, Jesus stood and cried, saying, If any man thirst, let him come unto me, and drink. He that believeth on me, as the scripture hath said, out of his belly shall flow rivers of living water. But this spake he of the Spirit, which they that believe on him should receive: for the Holy Ghost was not yet given; because that Jesus was not yet glorified" (John 7:37-39).

The gift of the Holy Sprit is the gift of a spiritual river of power that flows through our hearts, our homes, and our holding patterns. The gift of the Holy Spirit is the gift that makes winners of those who sometimes look like losers. President John F. Kennedy once said, "Success has many parents, but failure is an orphan that no one wants to adopt." He was right because people love winners who look like winners. Vince Lombardi, the famed and storied coach of the Green Bay Packers, once said, "Winning isn't everything; it's the only thing. I never even like to think that I have ever lost a football game—I just ran out of time before I could win." One writer said, "Most people admire a good loser as long as it's somebody other than themselves."

Passwords to Power

People love to win, but everything that looks like winning is not winning and everybody who looks like they are losing are not losing. Some years ago I heard about two football coaches who took a break from their routines and went north to do some ice fishing. They secured the required gear and fishing paraphernalia—lines, lures, rods, poles, and they borrowed a small power saw to cut holes through the ice. They hit the road and camped at what they perceived to be a great location. They proceeded to cut a hole in the ice but before they got started a strong voice interrupted them saying, "Stop. There are no fish under the ice." Startled by the voice, they looked at each other, and after assuring one another neither was insane, they went back to the task of cutting a hole in the ice. The voice spoke again, "Stop. There are no fish under the ice." They looked up. They thought the voice was coming from above, but they didn't see anybody. As their eyes scanned the vacant scenery, the voice thundered out again. "Stop. There are no fish under the ice." Finally one coach couldn't stand it any longer. He stood on his feet and cried out, "Lord is that You speaking to us?" The voice replied, "No. This is not the Lord. But I am the manager on duty of this ice skating arena that you are cutting up, and I repeat there are no fish under the ice."

What the coaches had labeled as ideal for fishing was, in reality, an arena that had absolutely nothing to do with fishing. The place in which the coaches had pitched their tents to go fishing had been designed for something else. In this life, the enemies of God's people fail to comprehend the reality that neither things nor circumstances prove to be what they seem. We are fed from a source the human eye can't see. Calvary was not what Calvary seemed to be to the eyes of our Lord's enemies. They looked at the cross and saw an end. God looked at the same cross and saw a new beginning for a new brand of blessings. The cross that meant death to some meant life to others.

There is a wonderful illustration of winners that seem to be losers in the 11th chapter of Hebrews. Abel, Enoch, Noah, Abraham, Sarah, Isaac, Jacob, Joseph, Moses, and Rahab all wear the badges of the blessed. However, verse 35 of Hebrews 11 introduces us to some winners that looked like losers:

"Women received their dead raised to life again: and others were tortured, not accepting deliverance; that they might obtain a better resurrection. And others had trial of cruel mockings and scourgings, yea, moreover of bonds and imprisonment: They were stoned, they were sawn asunder, were tempted, were slain with the sword: they wandered about in sheepskins and goatskins; being destitute, afflicted, tormented. (Of whom the world was not worthy) they wandered in deserts, and in mountains, and in dens and caves of the earth. And these all, having obtained a good report through faith, received not the promise. God having provided some better thing for us, that they without us should not be made perfect" (Hebrews 11:35-40).

We readily see the obvious victory where the writer says, "Women received their dead raised to life again," but there is an even greater victory as he says, "and others were tortured, not accepting deliverance; that they might obtain a better resurrection." None of these people would be viewed as "ready for prime time." They were not candidates for talk show invitations. They wouldn't appear on the cover of *People Magazine*. They were not delivered from the fiery furnace like the stalwart heroes in the Book of Daniel. They were not saved in the lions' den like Daniel and other special sons of destiny. As a matter of fact, these were victims of the lion's wrath. Torn flesh. Broken bones. Consumed organs. They were not raised from the dead like Lazarus of Bethany, yet the Bible says, "They obtained a better resurrection." Theirs was a better resurrection than Lazarus', because after Jesus raised Lazarus from the four-day grave in which he resided, Lazarus had to die again. After women received their dead back from the grave somebody had to return them to the grave again. However, when the saints died who were "tortured" and refused to recant their faith in a living Christ, they obtained a better resurrection. Why was it better? It was better because they never died again. It was better because they went home to live with God — "Absent from the body, present with the Lord." God did not fail them, and they did not disappoint God like Peter or betray Him like Judas. The world killed them, but the world did not stop them. They went home, "dropped their war tools and stuck their swords in the sandy banks of time."

They fastened their hands around victory palms to wave through out eternity. Losers? Not these. Their robes were washed white in the blood of the Lamb. The death dew had been wiped from their foreheads never to form again.

The Lord is with Us

"God is in the midst of her; she shall not be moved: God shall help her, and that right early. Be still, and know that I am God: I will be exalted among the heathen, I will be exalted in the earth. The Lord of hosts is with us; the God of Jacob is our refuge. Selah" (Psalm 46:5-7).

A.   The Lord keeps us safe for our good and His glory

The need to be safe and secure is a universal need, and the God of the universe is the only Source that is big enough to meet that massive need. As long as the people of God were connected to the loving presence of God, the city of Jerusalem was invincible. As long as their souls were anchored in their God, no enemy would prevail.

From time to time in northern waters, the wind blows and surface ice moves in the same direction in northern waters. The wind drives, and the waves and surface ice all bow to the pressure that the wind exerts, but icebergs care nothing for the force of the wind. Icebergs majestically move in the opposite direction because of the mass of the icebergs is safely hidden under the surface of the water and is caught in the strong currents that move them. Caught in the grip of a current beneath the water, the icebergs move in the current's direction regardless of how the wind blows. As long as we abide in the will of God, there is no force that can destroy us. There is no death that can claim us until our work is done. If we plan, pay, pray, and even play within the will of God, we are invincible until our work is done. When our work is done, it's time for a promotion. Although we are in the safety zone when we are in the will of God, we are also in need of daily prayer. The open grave of the Lord Jesus Christ provides us with our firmest hold on life after death and to be "absent from the body" results in being "present with the Lord." The presence we enjoy within the body is finite compared to the presence that awaits us.

B. The Lord best provides us with the answer for identity.

The need to be a unique person is one we all have. We need to be noticed and recognized as special. God made us this way, and we seek to express our identity in our dress, walk, talk, language, beliefs and even in our hobbies. Our identity needs suffer at times when we are compared to others, have our feelings rejected or minimized, and when we are ignored. The Bible teaches us:

"For as many as are led by the Spirit of God, they are the sons of God.

For ye have not received the spirit of bondage again to fear; but ye have received the Spirit of adoption, whereby we cry, Abba, Father. The Spirit itself beareth witness with our spirit, that we are the children of God: And if children, then heirs; heirs of God, and joint-heirs with Christ; if so be that we suffer with him, that we may be also glorified together. For I reckon that the sufferings of this present time are not worthy to be compared with the glory which shall be revealed in us. For the earnest expectation of the creature waiteth for the manifestation of the sons of God" (Romans 8:14-19).

Some years ago I learned of an African-American slave who was sold to a family in Alabama during the late 1600s. This slave never bowed in humiliation to the evil system. Whipped, abused, sold from plantation to plantation, he was somewhat like a dandelion—always rising above circumstances and surroundings. One day an overseer asked another why the slave could not be broken. The man replied, "I am told that he was the son of a king in Africa. He is our slave. He has been in slavery for years, but for some reason he can't seem to forget he was the son of a king."

Through the new birth, which takes place when parented by the Word of God and the Spirit of God, Christians enter into God's family with an adult standing. This adult status means we do not have to wait in order to enjoy the blessings of our inheritance. Led by the Spirit, loved by the Father, and likened unto the Son, we enter the Kingdom as newborns spiritually, but we have the status of adults. To fully appreciate the Christian's status with God, it is necessary to remember Paul is also speaking of the Christian as being adopted into the family of God.

The Roman adoption process was serious and detailed. It is viewed more seriously when we understand what the Romans called *patria potestas*, the absolute power of the father over the adopted child. No matter how old the child was, he never came of age; he was always under the possession and control of the father. In adoption, the adoptee had to pass from one *patria protestas* to another. When the process was completed, the adoptee lost all rights in his old family but gained all the rights of a completely legitimate son in his new family. He became heir to his new father's estate even if other sons were born. According to Roman law, the old life of the adoptee was completely wiped out. All legal debts were cancelled. The past had no hold on the adopted person who entered a new life. According to Roman law the adoptee was literally and legally the son of his new *patria potestas*. Roman history provides an insightful historical illustration of how binding Roman law was in the arena of adoption. The Roman Emperor Cladius adopted Nero so Nero could succeed him. They had no blood relationship. Claudius already had a daughter whose name was Octavia. To finalize the alliance Nero sought to marry Octavia. Even though they were not related by blood, Roman law decreed them to be brother and sister. A special Roman ordinance had to be passed by the senate before Nero and Octavia were allowed to be married.

Paul saw us before we became Christians. We were under the absolute control of our old sinful human nature but God looked beyond our faults and saw our needs. He brought us into His family and His holy kingdom. Past debts have been cancelled. We are now sons and daughters of the King. This solves our identity issues. Dressed up or dressed down, we are now royalty. Regardless of where we go or what we encounter, we are to face life as sons and daughters of the King. God help us all never to forget who we are. Face what you must, but keep in your head and your heart the fact your Father is the "King of all kings." The heathen might rage and kingdoms might move, but the Lord of hosts is with us. He is in our midst just as He is in the midst of the lampstands and the four and twenty elders in the Book of Revelation.

C. The Lord alone grants us meaning for eternity.

Deep within the human spirit, God has planted the need for us to have the events in our lives add up to something meaningful. We need to find a reason for being and have hope for the future. Kids write on walls. Lovers carve shapes of hearts on trees in order to send the message they are part of something that will last forever. The message we all seek to send is that we are involved in a process that enables us to stand in proud defiance of time and the seasons that time brings. Whether in a fraternity, sorority, secret order, or accepting public recognition, the human spirit seeks a confidence that will be constant and abiding amid the swift changes of time. God built into us a spirit that can communicate with His eternal Spirit, and therefore we seek the unperishable. We long for that which is unlike a vesture that shall one day be folded and put away. In 1882 Friedrick Nietzsche said, "God is dead. The dawn of science will be the doom of faith." He was wrong. The human body wears out, but the human spirit wears on.

Many years ago, at my beloved Selma University in Selma, Alabama, one of my classmates, Dr. Willie Muse, said, "If you find a rat laughing at a cat you can bank on the fact there is a hole somewhere close by." Even though the human body must bear the burdens of the years, the human spirit is only content when it lays hold of something that time cannot bear away. It is this grasp of forever that enables us to smile at the enemy that time can sometimes become.

(1) Thanks be to God the Gospel provides us with a message that is forever. When we believe the Gospel, we believe in something that is forever. "Jesus Christ is the same yesterday, today and forever" (Hebrews 13:8). "The eternal God is thy refuge, and underneath are the everlasting arms: And he shall thrust out the enemy from before thee; and shall say, destroy them" (Deuteronomy 33:27). "And, Thou, Lord, in the beginning hast laid the foundation of the earth; and the heavens are the works of thine hands; They shall perish; but thou remainest; and they all shall wax old as doth a garment; And as a

vesture shalt thou fold them up, and they shall be changed: but thou art the same, and thy years shall not fail" (Hebrews 1:10-12).

(2)   Thanks be to God that we can develop a relationship that will last forever. Across the years, I have learned every helpful relationship and friendship we establish is not designed by God to last beyond certain periods in our lives. God sends people into our lives at times for that time alone. There are some good friends who blessed us at a time when we really needed them, but they moved on after the need was met. If you can look back and smile, the relationship was not a waste of time, even if it no longer exists. Our lives are held firmly in God's love and grace. He is not One who is detached. We can, through Jesus Christ, have a relationship that outlasts all other relationships.

"Who shall separate us from the love of Christ? Shall tribulation, or distress, or persecution, or famine, or nakedness, or peril, or sword?

As it is written, For thy sake we are killed all the day long; we are accounted as sheep for the slaughter. Nay, in all these things we are more than conquerors through him that loved us. For I am persuaded, that neither death, nor life, nor angels, nor principalities, nor powers, nor things present, nor things to come. Nor height, nor depth, nor any other creature, shall be able to separate us from the love of God, which is in Christ Jesus our Lord" (Romans 8:33-39).

It is an uncomparable symbol granted to us by the Father that nothing in the entire garment of hurts, hazard, trials, and tragedies "can separate us from the love of God, which is in Christ Jesus our Lord." Nothing in time or eternity, nothing in heaven or hell, or the here and now, nor anything in the there and then can break the relationship that we can have with our Creator, who is also our Comforter. Our relationship with God is our imperishable treasure. Jesus says in John 17:3, "And this is life eternal, that they might know thee the only true God, and Jesus Christ, whom thou hast sent."

We can believe something can last forever, we can develop a relationship that lasts forever, and by God's death-defying grace, we can do something that can last forever. "And being in Bethany in the house of Simon the leper, as he sat at meat, there came a woman having an alabaster box of ointment of spikenard very precious; and she brake the box, and poured it on his head. And there were some that had indignation within themselves, and said, Why was this waste of the ointment made? For it might have been sold for more than three hundred pence, and have been given to the poor. And they murmured against her. And Jesus said, Let her alone; why trouble ye her? She hath wrought a good work on me. For ye have the poor with you always, and whensoever ye will ye may do them good: but me ye have not always. She hath done what she could; she is come aforehand to anoint my body to the burying" (Mark 14:3-8). Man's memory might be short, but God does not forget those who give because they lift up their values to His values. God refuses to permit any deed of love to be lost. Love lives forever because God will not forget. In the days of our Lord when any box of spikenard ointment was broken for a person of royal stature the entire box was used. No one else was worthy to receive any of that which was dedicated to royalty. The woman with whom Jesus spoke poured out the whole box. She gave it all to the One on His way to Calvary to give His all. Judas accused her of wastefulness, but Jesus said, "Verily I say unto you, Wheresoever this gospel shall be preached throughout the whole world, this also that she hath done shall be spoken of for a memorial of her" (Mark 14:9).

Long after the earth has passed away, what we have done and continue to do for Christ will last and live. As a matter of fact, *only* what we do for Christ will last and will live. Unlike Lot in the Book of Genesis, this woman put her hand and her heart to a work that will never perish.

"And he looked toward Sodom and Gomorrah, and toward all the land of the plain, and beheld, and, lo, the smoke of the country went up as the smoke of a furnace. And it came to pass, when God destroyed the cities of the plain, that God remembered Abraham, and sent Lot out of the midst of the overthrow, when he overthrew the cities in the which Lot dwelt" (Genesis 19:28-30).

Lot pitched his tent near Sodom and Gomorrah. He eventually sat at the gate of the city, meaning he assumed some formal governmental role as a policy maker. That everything Lot worked on and worked for one day went up in smoke is the tragedy. Our works will one day be tried by fire.

"Every man's work shall be made manifest: for the day shall declare it, because it shall be revealed by fire; and the fire shall try every man's work of what sort it is. If any man's work abide which he hath built thereupon, he shall receive a reward. If any man's work shall be burned, he shall suffer loss: but he himself shall be saved; yet so as by fire" (1 Corinthians 3:13-15). How sad it will be to accomplish nothing that will count in eternity. The best way to destroy a house is to attack it's foundation or build it out of cheap material. Cheap religion will go up in smoke at the last day. Works of love that have affected the steps we've taken, the moves we've made, and words we've spoken will live as long as God lives. Blessed be God the Father.

"For God is not unrighteous to forget your work and labour of love, which ye have shewed toward his name, in that ye have ministered to the saints, and do minister" (Hebrews 6:10).

Sick or well, shut in or shut out, overlooked or underappreciated, God will not forget our labors of love. Even though we live in a world where there is always someone else who is willing to work harder, stay longer, or stand closer to the flame, God does not grade on the curve. What we *are* steers what we *do*. There is nothing greater than love that we can apply to our work, and for God there is nothing less than love that we need to bring into our work with Him. God deals with each of us according to our own personal labor of love. We are not things, species, or ideas. We are people with different gifts and goals. God expects nothing from us but the best we can give. Don't compare yourself with others—God doesn't. Don't minimize your five barley loaves and two small fish (John 6:9)—God won't. Don't listen to what the devil told you about your limits—God didn't. The road less travelled is not the road *not* travelled. We are travelling a road where others, such as the widow who timidly made her way to the temple treasury and cast in her two mites, have traveled with success. Jesus said concerning her gift "of a truth I say unto you, that this poor widow hath cast in more than they all" (Luke 21:3).

On the road that leads to glory, the God we work for is the God we work with. In a time of war it's good to have the presence of the One who cannot lose and will never die. And now Lord, I thank You that You are Jehovah-Shammah. Pronounce it, say it, remember it, and live with it daily.

Chapter 7

AND NOW LORD
Pronounce Him as: Jehovah Raah

The Lord is My Shepherd

With God as our Shepherd, we see compassion matched with unmeasured power. In some cases we find compassion that has a cap on power and in other cases we witness massive power that is short on compassion. When we view God as Jehovah Raah we see in one source a heart overflowing with compassion for us and power that is able to protect us to the point that even when we "walk through the valley of the shadow of death," we have no need "to fear evil." The God who is able to keep us is the same One who wants to keep us. The God who can save us is the same God who wants to save us. The God who can heal is the same One who loves to heal. The idea of God as Shepherd speaks with blazing poignancy to the needs of needy people. What God brings us to, God will bring us through.

Speaking of Himself, Jesus says in John 10:7-18:

"Then said Jesus unto them again, Verily, verily, I say unto you, I am the door of the sheep. All that ever came before me are thieves and robbers: but the sheep did not hear them. I am the door: by me if any man enter in, he shall be saved, and shall go in and out, and find pasture. The thief cometh not, but for to steal, and to kill, and to destroy: I am come that they might have life, and that they might have it more abundantly. I am the good shepherd: the good shepherd giveth his life for the sheep. But he that is an hireling, and not the shepherd, whose own the sheep are not, seeth the wolf coming, and leaveth the sheep, and fleeth: and the wolf catcheth them, and scattereth the sheep. The hireling fleeth, because he is an hireling, and careth not for the sheep. I am the good shepherd, and know my sheep, and am known of mine. As the Father knoweth me, even so know I the Father: and I lay down my life for the sheep. And other sheep I have, which are not of this fold: them also I must bring, and they shall hear my voice; and there shall be one fold, and one shepherd. Therefore doth my Father love me, because I lay down my life, that I might take it again. No man taketh it from me, but I lay it down of myself. I have power to take it again. This commandment have I received of my Father."

This Shepherd-sheep relationship is one that forces us to look at ourselves in ways our pride protests. Sheep have some serious problems. Left to themselves sheep would literally eat themselves into a grave. Sheep need wise land management. The tooth formation of sheep causes them to uproot grass instead of clip it. Without the guidance of a shepherd who knows when to lead the sheep from one pasture to another sheep will create a barren field that eventually will become a death bed. As our Shepherd, God takes care of our failures, our foes, and our futures.

People who seek to harm God's people need to be warned. God has no sheep who are left without the protective intervention of an Almighty Shepherd. In this life none of us have all the wrinkles ironed out and all the problems solved but we take comfort in the fact that we have one who "sits high and looks low" and there is no failure in Him.

Defended by an Able Shepherd

In David, the Bible reveals the role of the shepherd as an able defender of his sheep. "And David said unto Saul, Thy servant kept his father's sheep, and there came a lion, and a bear, and took a lamb out of the flock: And I went out after him, and smote him, and delivered it out of his mouth: and when he arose against me, I caught him by his beard, and smote him, and slew him. Thy servant slew both the lion and the bear: and this uncircumcised Philistine shall be as one of them, seeing he hath defied the armies of the living God. David said moreover, The Lord that delivered me out of the paw of the lion, and out of the paw of the bear, he will deliver me out of the hand of this Philistine. And Saul said unto David, Go, and the Lord be with thee" (1 Samuel 17:34-37).

Watered by a Caring Shepherd

In Jacob, the flocks are watered by a Shepherd who finds for His sheep the necessity that they can't live without.

"And he looked, and behold a well in the field, and, lo, there were three flocks of sheep lying by it; for out of that well they watered the flocks: and a great stone was upon the well's mouth. And thither were all the flocks gathered: and they rolled the stone from the well's mouth, and watered the sheep, and put the stone again upon the well's mouth in his place. And Jacob said unto them, My brethren, whence be ye? And they said, of Haran are we. And he said unto them, know ye Laban the son of Nahor? And they said, we know him. And he said unto them, Is he well? And they said, He is well: and, behold, Rachel his daughter cometh with the sheep. And he said, Lo, it is yet high day, neither is it time that the cattle should be gathered together: water ye the sheep, and go and feed them. And they said, We cannot, until all the flocks be gathered together, and till they roll the stone from the well's mouth; then we water the sheep. And while he yet spake with them, Rachel came with her father's sheep: for she kept them. And it came to pass, when Jacob saw Rachel the daughter of Laban his mother's brother, and the sheep of Laban his mother's brother, that Jacob went near, and rolled the stone from the well's mouth, and watered the flock of Laban his mother's brother" (Genesis 29:2-10).

You have no need to feel insecure when you pronounce God as Jehovah Raah. The God who looks at you looks out for you. Whenever the Shepherd ushers you from a place, person, or position, it is a movement that has your highest good at the center. Don't be upset if the scenery looks less than desirable. There are always stones planted to conceal value. There are scarecrows stationed in fields that are ripe with harvest. As a Christian, you have a Shepherd who knows how and when to meet your needs far better than you do. He leads and He enables. The Bible tells us in Psalm 105:36-37: "He smote also all the firstborn in their land, the chief of all their strength.

He brought them forth also with silver and gold: and there was not one feeble person among their tribes."

The psalmist recalled the exodus of God's people from Egypt and he informs us "There was not one feeble person among their tribes." I find it amazing that when it was time to move out, God, in His mysterious providence, healed the people to the point that even the elderly walked out at His command. If God tells you to "take up your bed and walk," you can. If God calls you to "search for a city whose builder and maker is God," you can find it. If God permits the company to unjustly fire you, it is only because you have out-grown your usefulness and calling for that arena. Never forget—the God who gave you wings to fly will sometimes allow people to force you to use them. The Shepherd leads by different designs, but He always leads safely.

Sometimes God leads us in ways that will guarantee that we will learn more about Him and what praising Him can do for us and those we love. Psalm 8:2 says, "out of the mouth of babes and sucklings hast thou ordained strength because of thine enemies, that thou mightest still the enemy and the avenger." God as Jehovah Raah is so great a Shepherd that when satanic forces marshal its resources to attack us, the praise in the mouth of a small baby is sufficient to invite the power of the Almighty God. The cry of an infant is enough to reveal the glory of One who cannot fail. God needs no defense from us—just our praise—and if we praise Him, He will prevail and "still the enemy and the avenger."

A Securing Shepherd Knows the Way to Fat Pastures

"And they went to the entrance of Gedor, even unto the east side of the valley, to seek pasture for their flocks. And they found fat pasture and good, and the land was wide, and quiet, peaceable; for they of Ham had dwelt there of old. And these written by name came in the days of Hezekiah king of Judah, and smote their tents, and the habitations that were found there, and destroyed them utterly unto this day, and dwelt in their rooms: because there was pasture there for their flocks" (I Chronicles 4:39-41). This story speaks of the descendants of Simeon, a son of Jacob by Leah. He was held as a hostage by Joseph (Genesis 42:24) and denounced by Jacob (Genesis 34:30) because he joined Levi in the massacre of the Shechemites (Genesis 34:25-31).

Unlike the seed of Simeon, God doesn't have to search for fat pastures. God doesn't have to survey valleys or scout for quiet and peaceful real estate. God doesn't have to struggle to secure—He already has the deeds to every parcel of property in existence. If you will only work in cooperation with Him and follow His leadership according to His schedule you will become more than a conqueror. God rejoices in taking His people from the land of not enough to the pastures of more than enough.

The formula for entering into fat pastures:

(1) Work in cooperation with God (Genesis 3:19). God informed Adam, "In the sweat of thy face shalt thou eat bread."

(2) Follow God's leadership. "He maketh me to lie down in green pastures: He leadeth me beside the still water" (Psalm 23:2). Sheep are so easily frightened they will not drink from rushing waters but will from a quiet and peaceful pool. The God of creation is also the God of redemption. God knows the battles we have fought and won, and He knows the secret fears that dog our steps. People and sheep have a tendency to wander into unsafe places without the right kind of leadership. There are few things in this world that have caused as much torment, torture, and havoc as the presence of fear. In spite of strong affirmations of hope, fear has a way of eating away at the very fiber of our being.

I have seen people drive their partners away because of their fear of intimacy. I have witnessed parent-child relationships destroyed by the fear that a mistakes made will not be forgotten. Fear can be likened to contracting a disease that weakens both resistance and ability. Have you ever wondered why the Bible speaks to us to "fear not" so often? It is because God knows in spite of our boasts of courage, deep within our sinful nature we are fearful beings. We are fearful of being overlooked, left alone, and left out. Many times we run into people who are stand-offish. They sometimes seem to generate a posture of being superior. The real truth behind this kind of behavior is often rooted in fear. Many who keep others at a distance do so because they are afraid they are not impressive close up. The people who act as if they are better may, in reality, fear they are not as good.

In my book *Climbing the Sacred Ladder*, I speak to what is called "Foolish Fear with Power."

"Those who are victims of foolish fear and have positions of power become very dangerous. This is true because fear often breeds persecution by those who have the power to persecute the objects of their fear. Fear born of wisdom creates a soul open to inspiration, but foolish fear results in a dangerous insecurity. History is replete with examples of persecution motivated by fear.

At one time, witchcraft was blamed for all misfortunes people could not explain. Whenever a person experienced an illness, crop failure, sudden death, severe depression, or any form of mental illness, it was assumed a witch had cast a spell. Some believed "witches could make cows go dry by stealing their milk or casting a spell on a churn to prevent butter from forming. People also thought witches could raise storms, ruin crops, and turn people into animals." This fear eventually brought forth unbelievable persecution. Some historians believe between 1484 and 1872 more than three hundred thousand women were put to death because they were labeled as witches. Many were tortured to such a degree they confessed to being a witch to avoid further punishment. According to the *World Book Encyclopedia*, people used many kinds of tests to determine whether a woman was a witch. For example, they looked for moles, scars, or other marks on a woman's body where a pin could be stuck without causing pain. Such devil's marks were said to be places where the devil had touched the accused woman. Devil's marks also included birth marks. In another test, "people tied the suspected woman's arms and legs and threw her into deep water. If she floated she was considered guilty of being a witch. If she drowned, she was innocent." As you can see, the test was deadly. A woman might be found innocent although the test itself killed her. Foolish fear with power is dangerous!"

God sees the cost of our fears. He knows the price we and others have to pay for them, and He speaks to us as Jehovah Raah says, "Fear not" (2 Timothy 1:7). "For God hath not given us the spirit of fear; but of power, and of love, and of a sound mind" (1 John 4:18). "There is no fear in love; but perfect love casteth out fear: because fear hath torment. He that feareth is not made perfect in love." "Yea, though I walk through the valley of shadow of death, I will fear no evil; for thou art with me; thy rod and thy staff they comfort me" (Psalm 23:4). "The Lord is my light and my salvation: whom shall I fear? The Lord is the strength of my life: of whom shall I be afraid?" (Psalm 27:1). "The Lord is on my side; I will not fear: what can man do unto me?" (Psalm 118:6). "And he (Jesus) said unto them, Why are ye so fearful? How is it that ye have no faith?" (Mark 4:40). "In God have I put my trust; I will not be afraid what man can do unto me." (Psalms 56:11). "Behold, God is my salvation; I will trust, and not be afraid" (Isaiah 12:2). According to God's schedule, the people who get to the top don't fall to the top. They get there by hard work, overcoming hard times, and patiently waiting for the right time. God is not only a God of planning—He is also a God of perfect timing. God scatters us as He judges us and labels our deficits. Yet He does not sweep us away in His wrath. When the Bible speaks of God scattering the proud it uses the Greek verb disaskoopize. Diaskoopize not only means "to scatter," it also mean "to winnow." During biblical days when the harvesters winnowed the grain, they tossed a shovel full in the air so the wind would carry away the chaff (husk) but leave the kernel. It takes time for us to get rid of stuff we don't need for future assignments. Through the process of time, God scatters from us not only the unnecessary but also the self-defeating things that could abort His wonderful plans for our future. God sometimes uses adverse winds to teach us He is not as impressed about what we achieve as He is about whom we adore.

The Word of God tells us in Psalm 37:4: "Delight thyself in the Lord and He will give thee the desires of thine heart." It takes time to walk with God to the point you will delight in Him, but as you delight in God's presence, your heart will begin to have the right kind of desires. As you grow closer to God, your desires will become too big to be controlled by situations and/or circumstances. Through the process of time, the heart on the inside becomes greater than the events and possessions on the outside regardless of the worldly value placed on those events or possessions.

"And Jesus entered and passed through Jericho. And, behold, there was a man named Zacchaeus, which was the chief among the publicans, and he was rich. And he sought to see Jesus who he was; and could not for the press, because he was little of stature. And he ran before, and climbed up into a sycamore tree to see him: for he was to pass that way. And when Jesus came to the place, he looked up, and saw him, and said unto him, Zacchaeus, make haste, and come down; for today I must abide at thy house. And he made haste, and came down, and received him joyfully. And when they saw it, they all murmured, saying, That he was gone to be guest with a man that is a sinner. And Zacchaeus stood, and said unto the Lord; Behold, Lord, the half of my goods I give to the poor; and if I have taken any thing from any man by false accusation, I restore him fourfold. And Jesus said unto him, this day is salvation come to this house, forsomuch as he also is a son of Abraham. For the Son of man is come to seek and to save that which was lost" (Luke 19:1-10).

Before our Lord went home with him, Zacchaeus had been a man ruled by wealth. The Romans used him to collect taxes, and he used the Romans by making himself rich as he gouged his fellow Jews. To the people, Zacchaeus was a turncoat. To the Romans, he was a tool they used to finance their worldwide empire as they levied unjust taxes on all of the nations under their control. Jesus spoke to Zacchaeus as he hung on the limb of a sycamore tree because Jesus knew one day the limb Zacchaeus was sitting on would break. When the limb broke, everything the limb was holding would fall.

Jesus didn't wave His hand from the ground or try to cast some spell on Zacchaeus. He took the time to go home with him. I don't know how long it took, but I know Jesus took all the time that was needed to create in him a new heart, and the new heart on the inside became greater to Zacchaeus than all the money he had made on the outside. By giving to the poor and making restitution, Zacchaeus won something money could not buy. He reached the point where he understood that in order to become something better, he had to become something different, and Jesus built the bridge that enabled him to make the transition. No earthly power could have brought Zacchaeus to the place of repentance and restitution. Somehow the grace of God supplied through faith something he could never gain through power. We don't have to fight unprotected or work unequipped. We don't have to suffer unrewarded or serve unprepared. We serve a God who, after He changes us from the inside, can take us through the fire unharmed and lead us through deep waters and keep us from drowning. Time is a price we each must pay if we are to gain the power we need to defeat evil and outlast setbacks, suffering, sorrow, and sin. In spite of our ability to gain a lot with a little time, in certain regions of our lives there are no shortcuts or time-saving measures that will nullify the need for our time investment with God. We must align our purposes with God, and we must set our timepieces according to His master schedule.

Some time ago some very clever thieves broke into a department store. They didn't take anything out of the store during the time of the break in. They simply went through the store and changed the price tags. They put cheap tags on expensive items such as televisions, cameras, kitchen appliances, jewelry, and clothing. Almost four hours went by before management discovered what had been done. Some people literally got some steals. That incident dramatically illustrates a satanic ploy. Some price tags have been changed. Some are paying too much for what they are getting and some are trying to purchase cheaply that which will never go on sale. Abraham had to spend twenty-five years with God as a man of faith before Isaac, the son of promise, was born. Joseph had God-given dreams of greatness as a lad. He was 17 when he arrived in Egypt as slave. It was not until he reached 30 he became a ruler second only to Pharaoh. Moses at 40 was ready to assume his role as emancipator for his people, but it took forty more years before God saw him as fit to confront Pharaoh. God works in us during seasons of isolation in order to bring us to places of promotion.

Thou art with Me: Psalm 23

David used the first person to describe his journey with God:

Verse 2 - He maketh me to lie down in green pastures

Verse 2 - He leadeth me beside the still waters

Verse 3 - He restoreth my soul; He leadeth me in the path of righteousness for his name's sake.

After death entered the picture he says, "yea, though I walk through the valley of the shadow of death, I will fear no evil: For thou art with me."

What happened specifically to place death into this setting and color it with shades that only death could paint, we are not told. The psalmist might have felt an intense pain he had never known before. He could have had his thoughts interrupted by a funeral march. The memory of someone close to him who might have crossed the line between time and eternity may have gripped him so he felt acutely his own mortality. Also, the fear of running from King Saul may have been why David wrote this psalm. Whatever it was, it transformed his speech *about* God *toward* God. Anything that brings us to a point where we speak to God is something that works together for our good.

I recall from years ago the story about a young minister and an elderly man of God. They both quoted the 23rd Psalm. The young man's voice was clear and eloquent. When he finished the audience rewarded him with a standing ovation. Then the elderly minister spoke. Some cried tears, and some applauded through their tears, while the glory of the Lord filled the place where they were gathered. Someone defined the difference by saying "the young man knew the Psalm. The elderly man knew the Shepherd."

A canary dealer developed a unique way to teach domestic canaries to sing the songs that made the canaries from the Hartz Mountains of Germany famous. He first recorded the mesmerizing songs of the canaries from Germany. He then covered the cages of the domesticated birds with a cloth so thick it shut out all light. He then replayed for them the recorded songs of the famous canaries. In the dark, domesticated birds learned to listen, learned to focus, and learned to sing with a sweetness they could never have attained during the daylight. Anything that brings us closer to God will prove to work together for our good. There are some songs we only learn in this life's dark times. When life is buzzing, when we are lighthearted, when it is summertime and the living is easy we often don't take time to listen to God. When life's sun is set in some sorrow, God gets our attention, and in the darkness the Lord teaches us some lessons we need to learn in order to avoid becoming casualties in the war between good and evil.

The next time you find yourself in a cage in the dark, look up and say, "Thou art with me; I will fear no evil." It doesn't matter if it's a sick bed, a cemetery, a ride that is late showing up, or one that is never coming. It doesn't matter if the ride is late and you are early, or if the ride is early and you are late. It doesn't matter if you are ahead all alone or if you are behind all by yourself. Say, "Thou art with me," and you will find yourself fearing no evil.

Hard times don't nullify God's promises. Scandals come and go. Some men live and lie. All men live and die. God never misplaces His promises. People might change. Health might fade, but God never falls asleep on the job. Trouble comes to all of us. Satan seeks to use the trouble to short-circuit God's ministry, but God is Almighty and He will use the same trouble to serve as the cover where you will learn heavenly songs.

Joseph was 39 when his family entered Egypt as bewildered refugees. He lived for 71 years after their arrival and died at 110. At the death of Joseph, the Israelite's fortunes hit the bottom. Times were hard, but God had made a promise. He did not fall asleep. Even during tough times, the people were multiplied according to His schedule. God sent an emancipator crying, "Let my people go."

Moses had spent 40 years in the wilderness, but God knew where to find him, and He always knows where you are. God never loses an address, and He never forgets a name. God never makes a mistake. There is something immensely comforting in knowing that God knows all about you and loves you. What comfort there is in knowing the God who tracks the pathways of a hundred billion stars in each of a hundred million galaxies knows all about us. In all of our comings and goings by land, sea, and air God knows exactly where to find us and touches us just when we need it most.

God will meet our needs because He is the same God who sent Jesus Christ, his only begotten Son, into a world like this to save people like us. God's gift of Jesus proves He can be trusted to put food on our tables, clothes on our backs, shoes on our feet, and a roof over our heads. Jesus taught us to pray, "Give us this day our daily bread." In 1947 when the Dead Sea Scrolls were found, they also found the Greek word that the new testament uses in the model prayer for daily. The word was found on what proved to be a daily shopping list. It always referred to perishable items that had to be purchased or secured each day. They had no refrigerators or ice chests, therefore they could not stockpile or freeze foods for another day. God's grace is a daily need, and just as He supplies us with daily grace we can trust Him to supply us with our daily bread regardless of where we happen to be. If you have the passion to watch while God works, and listen when God speaks, He will give you the strength to overcome when necessary and outlast when required.

A minor league baseball player was playing in his first game in center field. The young man made 2 errors. His manager threw a fit. He leaped out of the dugout and called a time out. The manager then ran to center field, screamed at the player and said, "You can't catch a cold. Go over to the bench, sit down. Watch me and I'll show you how to play center field." The manager took the player's glove and called for the umpire to resume the game. The first hitter hit a high fly to center field. The ball got lost in the sun, hit the manager in the head and a runner scored. The second batter hit a shot between first and second base. The manager ran to his left and collided with the right fielder. The right fielder was the team's best hitter, but after his collision with the manager, the right fielder was so injured he had to be taken out of the game. The third batter hit a monstrous line drive that hit the manager between the eyes and knocked him out cold. When he regained his consciousness they put the manager on a stretcher and carried him off the field. As he passed the dugout the manager saw the young player he had replaced and said, "You make me sick! Do you have any idea of what you have done? You got center field so messed up nobody can play out there!" It's sad but it is true we live in a world where people will not only blame you for your minor mistakes, but they will seek to make you feel guilty for their major mistakes. It is amazing how often we see this blame game in the Bible.

1, Adam blamed God and Eve for his transgressions. (Genesis 3:12)
2. Eve blamed the serpent. (Genesis 3:13)
3. Aaron blamed the fire for the idol. (Exodus 32:24)
4. The servant with one talent blamed his lord for his failure. (Matthew 25:24-25)

First Kings 20:40 gives one of the best illustrations of this issue in the Bible. In this passage of Scripture, there is a revealing example of an admission of guilt. A man was given the task of keeping watch over a prisoner. The man allowed the prisoner to escape. When confronted by the king, the man who had been given the task replied, "As thy servant was busy here and there, he was gone. And the king of Israel said unto him, So shall thy judgment be; thyself hast decided it."

The man had been given the assignment of watching. However, he became involved in matters other than the task placed into his hands. He was busy. He says in his own defense he was "busy here and there." He was active. He was involved. He was a functioning, operative, assiduous, energetic, and dynamic man, but he failed at his task because his efforts were misdirected. The activities engaged "here and there" did not complete the task of his assignment. The busy man knew the seriousness of his task. He had been informed, "Keep this man: If by any means he be missing, then shall thy life be for his life, or else thou shalt pay a talent of silver" (v. 39). A talent of silver in today's currency would amount to $5,280. He failed at his task and the cost for failure was severe for him.

The Sheep Belong to the Shepherd

The need to belong is universal. When this need is met the development of self-esteem is realized. For nearly fifty years Frederick Douglass stood out as the chief intellectual voice of Black America. He was a primary figure in the abolitionist movement and continued to demand full rights for freedmen after slavery was abolished. He published the newspaper, *The North Star* from 1847 to 1864. He served as a U.S. Marshall in 1877, and in 1881 he was U.S. Minister to Haiti and Santo Domingo. Douglass shared a famous literary piece that revealed a portion of his childhood that provides a profound illustration of the worth of belonging. The experience involved him as a child, his mother, and a rather mean-spirited person he called Aunt Katy. Aunt Katy was the cook for the old slaveowner of the plantation where Douglass lived as a child. One morning she decided to punish young Frederick for something he had done. She forced him to go without food for a whole day, and on top of being forced to go hungry, she additionally required he watch the other children eat.

That night Frederick lay awake, hunger pangs preventing sleep. In his distress he went outside, stole an ear of corn, and roasted it in the flickering ashes of a smoldering fire. That same night, Frederick's mother made a rare visit. She was a slave on a farm about 20 miles down the road, and during Douglass' lifetime, was able to visit only a handful of times, always at night. That night she came to his aid. He told her about Aunt Katy's meanness. His mother called Aunt Katy, and after she tongue lashed her, Frederick's mother took the ear of corn from him and exchanged it with a generously large ginger cake.

Speaking of that night as a man Frederick Douglass said, "On that night I learned the fact that I was not only a child, I was somebody's child." With the dawn of a new morning she was gone, but the impression she made upon him undergirded him for the rest of his life. It gave him strength and a central theme around which he could live his life.

God wants no less for you. As a Christian, you are not only a sheep; you are somebody's sheep, and that somebody is the Great Shepherd.

"And when the chief Shepherd shall appear, ye shall receive a crown of glory that fadeth not away" (1 Peter 5:4).

In the same chapter, Peter goes on to say, "Humble yourselves therefore under the mighty hand of God, that he may exalt you in due time: Casting all your care upon him; for he careth for you" (v. 7).

No disease, devil, or destroyer can change the fact you are somebody's child, somebody's sheep, somebody's object of affection. Our times are in God's hand. God's Word is still true, and His promises are always good. The pains you feel, the needs you have, the things you suffer and the problems you face can never defeat the Almighty Power of the undying Shepherd "who was, who is and who is to come." Meditate on these words: "And there arose a great storm of wind, and the waves beat into the ship, so that it was now full. And he (Jesus) was in the hinder part of the ship, asleep on a pillow: and they awake him, and say unto him, master, carest thou not that we perish?" (Mark 4:37-38). "Be merciful unto me. O God, be merciful unto me:/for my soul trusteth in thee: yea, in the shadow of thy wings will I make my refuge, until these calamities be overpast" (Psalm 57:1).

"I had fainted, unless I believed to see the goodness of the Lord in the land of the living. Wait on the Lord; be of good courage, and he shall strengthen thine heart; wait, I say, on the Lord" (Psalm 27:13-14). "And we know that all things work together for good to them that love God, to them who are the called according to his purpose. If God be for us, who can be against us?" (Romans 8:28, 31). "greater is he that is in you, than he that is in the world" (1 John 4:4).

The Sheep's Victory

"Thou preparest a table before me in the presence of mine enemies: thou anointest my head with oil; my cup runneth over. Surely goodness and mercy shall follow me all the days of my life: and I will dwell in the house of the Lord forever" (Psalm 23:5-6).

In the very presence of an open enemy the Lord prepares a table where His sheep can dine. A cup that is running over symbolizes God's goal for our lives. God doesn't simply want you to cope—He invites you to flourish, and He is able to make it happen. When you trust in God's hands, He will bring your situation to the conclusion that is best for you and for those whose hearts are open to the leadership and the intervention of the Holy Spirit. This truth is dramatically revealed in Acts 16:6-34: "Now when they had gone throughout Phrygia and the region of Galatia, and were forbidden of the Holy Ghost to preach the word in Asia. After they were come to Mysia, they assayed to go into Bithynia: but the Spirit suffered them not. And they passing by Mysia came down to Troas. And a vision appeared to Paul in the night; There stood a man of Macedonia, and prayed him, saying, Come over into Macedonia, and help us. And after he had seen the vision, immediately we endeavored to go into Macedonia, assuredly gathering that the Lord had called us for to preach the gospel unto them. Therefore loosing from Troas, we came with a straight course to Samothracia, and the next day to Neapolis;/And from thence to Philippi, which is the chief city of that part of Macedonia, and a colony: and we were in that city abiding certain days. And on the sabbath we went out of the city by a river side, where prayer was wont to be made; and we sat down, and spake unto the women which resorted thither. And a certain woman named Lydia, a seller of purple, of the city of Thyatira, which worshipped God, heard us: whose heart the Lord opened, that she attended unto the things which were spoken of Paul. And when she was baptized, and her household, she besought us, saying, If ye have judged me to be faithful to the Lord, come into my house, and abide there. And she constrained us. And it came to pass, as we went to prayer, a certain damsel possessed with a spirit of divination met us, which brought her masters much gain by soothsaying. The same followed Paul and us, and cried, saying, These men are the servants of the most high God, which shew unto us the way of salvation. And this did she many days. But Paul, being grieved, turned and said to the spirit, I command thee in the name of Jesus Christ to come out of her. And he came out the same hour. And when her masters saw that the hope of their gains was gone, they caught

Paul and Silas, and drew them into the marketplace unto the rulers, And brought them to the magistrates, saying, These men, being jews, do exceedingly trouble our city. And teach customs, which are not lawful for us to receive, neither to observe, being Romans. And the multitude rose up together against them: and the magistrates rent off their clothes, and commanded to beat them. And when they had laid many stripes upon them, they cast them into prison, charging the jailer to keep them safely. Who, having received such a charge, thrust them into the inner prison, and made their feet fast in the stocks. And at midnight Paul and Silas prayed, and sang praises unto God: and the prisoners heard them. And suddenly there was a great earthquake, so that the foundations of the prison were shaken: and immediately all the doors were opened, and every one's bands were loosed. And the keeper of the prison waking out of his sleep, and seeing the prison doors open, he drew out his sword, and would have killed himself, supposing that the prisoners had been fled. But Paul cried with a loud voice, saying, Do thyself no harm. Then he called for a light, and sprang in, and came trembling, and fell down before Paul and Silas. And brought them out, and said, Sirs, what must I do to be saved? And they said, Believe on the Lord Jesus Christ, and thou shalt be saved, and thy house. And they spake unto him the word of the Lord, and to all that were in his house. And he took them the same hour of the night, and washed their stripes; and was baptized, he and all his, straightway. And when he had brought them into his house, he set meat before them, and rejoiced, believing in God with all his house."

Everyone involved whose hearts were open to God's leadership was blessed.

(1) The prisoners in the jail saw what prayer could do.

(2) Paul and Silas saw God raise the roof on their behalf.

(3) The jailer and his whole family were saved.

(4) The girl used to tell fortunes stopped being a plaything for playboys to play with.

(5) Lydia and her household was baptized, and God gave her a spiritual family in Philippi.

Paul was a philosopher. Lydia was a business woman. The demon-possessed girl was a victim of the occult. The jailer had been a prime candidate for suicide.

The God of victory gave them all a victory even as He gave them to each other.

On the road that leads to glory, the God we work for is the God we work with. In a time of war it's good to have the presence of the One who cannot lose and will never die. And now Lord, I thank You that You are Jehovah-Raah—pronounce it, say it, remember it, and live with it daily.

Chapter 8

AND NOW LORD
Pronounce Him As: Jehovah-Jireh

The Lord Will Provide

Genesis 22:14

"And Abraham called the name of that place Jehovah-Jireh: As it is said to this day, in the mount of the Lord it shall be seen."

The 22nd chapter of Genesis begins with the words "And it came to pass after these things, that God did tempt Abraham, and said unto him, Abraham: and he said, Behold here I am."

I find it amazing that the Holy Spirit teaches us so much with the simple phrase, "after these things." What are the things that led up to this most powerful and important chapter in the Bible? What are the things that serve as the forerunner of this prophetical portrait of the grace of God? What are the things that make a man ready to sacrifice the child of his old age and the child if his divine covenant with God. What are the things used to fashion a faith strong enough to portray the love of God the Father?

(1) Abraham sacrificed his father's house.

"Now the Lord had said unto Abram, Get thee out of thy country, and from thy kindred, and from thy father's house, unto a land that I will shew thee: And I will make of thee a great nation, and I will bless thee, and make thy name great; and thou shalt be a blessing: And I will bless them that bless thee, and curse him that curseth thee: and in thee shall all families of the earth be blessed. So Abram departed, as the Lord had spoken unto him; and Lot went with him: and Abram was seventy and five years old when he departed out of Haran. And Abram took Sarai his wife, and Lot his brother's son, and all their substance that they had gathered, and the souls that they had gotten in Haran; and they went forth to go into the land of Canaan; and into the land of Canaan they came" (Genesis 12:1-5).

(2) He sacrificed the well-watered plains of Jordan.

"And the land was not able to bear them, that they might dwell together: for their substance was great, so that they could not dwell together. And there was a strife between the herdsmen of Abram's cattle and the herdsmen of Lot's cattle: and the Canaanite and the Perizzite dwelled then in the land. And Abram said unto Lot, Let there be no strife, I pray thee, between me and thee, and between my herdsmen and thy herdsmen; for we be brethren. Is not the whole land before thee? separate thyself, I pray thee, from me: if thou wilt take the left hand, then I will go to the right; or if thou depart to the right hand, then I will go to the left. And Lot lifted up his eyes, and beheld all the plain of Jordan, that it was well watered every where, before the Lord destroyed Sodom and Gomorrah, even as the garden of the Lord, like the land of Egypt, as thou comest unto Zoar. Then Lot chose him all the plain of Jordan; and Lot journeyed east: and they separated themselves the one from the other.

Abram dwelled in the land of Canaan, and Lot dwelled in the cities of the plain, and pitched his tent toward Sodom. But the men of Sodom were wicked and sinners before the Lord exceedingly" (Genesis 13:6-13).

(3) He sacrificed gifts from the grateful king of Sodom.

"And the king of Sodom went out to meet him after his return from the slaughter of Chedorlaomer, and of the kings that were with him, at the valley of Shaveh, which is the king's dale. And Melchizedek king of Salem brought forth bread and wine: and he was the priest of the most high God. And he blessed him, and said, Blessed be Abram of the most high God, possessor of heaven and earth: And blessed be the most high God, which hath delivered thine enemies into thy hand. And he gave him tithes of all. And the king of Sodom said unto Abram, Give me the persons, and take the goods to thyself. And Abram said to the king of Sodom, I have lift up mine hand unto the Lord, the most high God, the possessor of heaven and earth. That I will not take from a thread even to a shoelatchet, and that I will not take any thing that is thine, lest thou shouldest say, I have made Abram rich: Save only that which the young men have eaten, and the portion of the men which went with me, Aner, Eshcol, and Mamre; let them take their portion" (Genesis 14:17-24).

(4)   He sacrificed Ishmael at God's directive.

"And the Lord visited Sarah as he had said, and the Lord did unto Sarah as he had spoken. For Sarah conceived, and bare Abraham a son in his old age, at the set time of which God had spoken to him. And Abraham called the name of his son that was born unto him, whom Sarah bare to him, Isaac. And Abraham circumcised his son Isaac being eight days old, as God had commanded him. And Abraham was an hundred years old, when his son Isaac was born unto him. And Sarah said, God hath made me to laugh, so that all that hear will laugh with me. And she said, Who would have said unto Abraham, that Sarah should have given children suck? for I have born him a son in his old age. And the child grew, and was weaned: and Abraham made a great feast the same day that Isaac was weaned. And Sarah saw the son of Hagar the Egyptian, which she had born unto Abraham, mocking. Wherefore she said unto Abraham, Cast out this bondwoman and her son: for the son of this bondwoman shall not be heir with my son, even with Isaac. And the thing was very grievous in Abraham's sight because of his son. And God said unto Abraham, Let it not be grievous in thy sight because of the lad, and because of thy bondwoman; in all that Sarah hath said unto thee, hearken unto her voice; for in Isaac shall thy seed be called. And also of the son of the bondwoman will I make a nation, because he is thy seed. And Abraham rose up early in the morning, and took bread, and a bottle of water, and gave it unto Hagar, putting it on her shoulder, and the child, and sent her away: and she departed, and wandered in the wilderness of Beer sheba." (Genesis 21:1-14).

The sacrifices made by Abraham prepared him for the test on Mount Moriah. *Moriah* means "Foreseen of God [Jehovah]." God foresaw the test long before Abraham made the first sacrifice. At the age of seventy-five God called Abram from his father's house and promised him a son through Sarah, his aged wife. God waited 25 years before he honored his promise of a son through Sarah. God then waited at least another 15 years before He summoned Abraham to Mount Moriah. We can clearly see that God spent at least forty years maturing Abraham's faith before He said:

"Take now thy son, thine only son Isaac, whom thou lovest, and get thee into the land of Moriah; and offer him there for a burnt offering upon one of the mountains which I will tell thee of" (Genesis 22:2).

With each sacrifice Abraham learned how to depend on God and scale the mountains that he faced. So it is with you, beloved. God is getting you ready to be shown off. God loves to show off His special vessels. The pride we have as earthly parents over our children's achievement pales in comparison to the heavenly pride God feels as we grow in grace and mature in faith. We get a glimpse of the pride of our Lord in us as we grow in Him, through a parable shared by Jesus in Luke 12:35-37:

"Let your loins be girded about, and your lights burning;/And ye yourselves like unto men that wait for their lord, when he will return from the wedding; that when he cometh and knocketh, they may open unto him immediately. Blessed are those servants, whom the lord when he cometh shall find watching: verily I say unto you, that he shall gird himself, and make them to sit down to meat, and will come forth and serve them."

Because the servants were ready, the master went into action. He was so pleased, so thrilled, that he reversed their roles. The master was so proud he became a servant to his servants. He was so impressed by what they had done he made them sit at the feast table while he waited upon them! I don't know about you, but I get goosebumps thinking that God can become so proud of me that He will bring my tea and serve my supper. In ways beyond our finite apprehension, the Lord is Jehovah-Jireh.

Nothing just happens. There is a plan, a purpose and a pattern. God's plan is to reclaim you. God's purpose is to prepare you for your good and His glory. God's pattern is to prepare you step by step, sacrifice by sacrifice, and even stop by stop along the way. God so leads you that you learn to walk by faith and lean upon Him alone. God so directs your steps that you reach a place in your life where you no longer consider the family and friends you love to be your first responsibility. However, it should never be forgotten that those who love God first loved others best. If God doesn't do much for your love, you limit Him in doing much for the rest of your resources. To have eloquence is to have great power over the minds, spirits, and imaginations of others. But love is greater than intellectual eminence. As a matter of fact, one of the most dangerous things in the world is knowledge without love—intellectual achievement without a serious concern for the good of others. An uneducated thief might steal a loaf of bread but an educated thief will steal the whole bakery.

The Bible teaches:

"Now faith is the substance of things hoped for, the evidence of things not seen. For by it the elders obtained a good report. Through faith we understand that the worlds were framed by the word of God, so that things which are seen were not made of things which do appear. By faith Abel offered unto God a more excellent sacrifice than Cain, by which he obtained witness that he was righteous, God testifying of his gifts: and by it he being dead yet speaketh. By faith Enoch was translated that he should not see death; and was not found, because God had translated him: for before his translation he had this testimony, that he pleased God. But without faith it is impossible to please him; for he that cometh to God must believe that he is, and that he is a rewarder of them that diligently seek him" (Hebrews 11:1-6).

Hope without love can be treacherous. Hope can become the mother of many of our mistakes. The word *hope* means "to open the eyes wide and watch for what is to come." Hope that is not built on Jesus' blood and righteousness can become the process of peril. Some seem to live as if they have no day of judgement to face. Some treat others cruelly and seem to hope that they can crawl into a hole in the ground and pull a rock over their heads and enjoy a restful sleep when this life is over. That kind of hope tempts multitudes to self deceitfulness. That kind of hope is a fawning traitor of right thinking and a deceiver that only promises a peace that it knows it cannot deliver.

The hope that is filled with the love of God is the only hope that serves as a never-failing minister of strength, elevation and inspiration. God did not give up on Abraham in spite of his faults and failures. God did not write him off in spite of his detours and defeats. Abraham moved out at God's command. Abraham took Lot, his nephew, with him and Lot created some serious problems for Abraham until they agreed to separate. Abraham took Sarai and a preconceived unholy agreement with him when he left Ur, and that agreement got both of them in trouble on two different occasions.

A. The agreement

"And it came to pass, when God caused me to wander from my father's house, that I said unto her, This is thy kindness which thou shalt shew unto me; at every place whither we shall come, say of me, He is my brother" (Genesis 20:13).

B.   Trouble in Egypt with Pharaoh

"And there was a famine in the land: and Abram went down into Egypt to sojourn there; for the famine was grievous in the land. And it came to pass, when he was come near to enter into Egypt, that he said unto Sarai his wife, Behold now, I know that thou art a fair woman to look upon: Therefore it shall come to pass, when the Egyptians shall see thee, that they shall say, This is his wife: and they will kill me, but they will save thee alive. Say, I pray thee, thou art my sister: that it may be well with me for thy sake; and my soul shall live because of thee. And it came to pass, that, when Abram was come into Egypt, the Egyptians beheld the woman that she was very fair. The princes also of Pharaoh saw her, and commended her before Pharaoh:

and the woman was taken into Pharaoh's house. And he entreated Abram well for her sake: and he had sheep, and oxen, and he asses, and menservants, and maidservants, and she asses, and camels. And the Lord plagued Pharaoh and his house with great plagues because of Sarai Abram's wife. And Pharaoh called Abram, and said, What is this that thou hast done unto me? why didst thou not tell me that she was thy wife? Why saidst thou, She is my sister? so I might have taken her to me to wife: now therefore behold thy wife, take her, and go thy way. And Pharaoh commanded his men concerning him: and they sent him away, and his wife, and all that he had" (Genesis 12:10-20).

C. Trouble in Gerar with king Abimelech

"And Abraham journeyed from thence toward the south country, and dwelled between Kadesh and Shur, and sojourned in Gerar. And Abraham said of Sarah his wife, She is my sister: and Abimelech king of Gerar sent, and took Sarah. But God came to Abimelech in a dream by night, and said to him, Behold, thou art but a dead man, for the woman which thou hast taken; for she is a man's wife. But Abimelech had not come near her: and he said, Lord, wilt thou slay also a righteous nation? Said he not unto me, She is my sister? and she, even she herself said, He is my brother: in the integrity of my heart and innocency of my hands have I done this. And God said unto him in a dream, Yea, I know that thou didst this in the integrity of thy heart; for I also withheld thee from sinning against me: therefore suffered I thee not to touch her. Now therefore restore the man his wife; for he is a prophet, and he shall pray for thee, and thou shalt live: and if thou restore her not, know thou that thou shalt surely die, thou, and all that are thine. Therefore Abimelech rose early in the morning, and called all his servants, and told all these things in their ears: and the men were sore afraid. Then Abimelech called Abraham, and said unto him, What hast thou done unto us? and what have I offended thee, that thou hast brought on me and on my kingdom a great sin? thou hast done deeds unto me that ought not to be done. And Abimelech said unto Abraham, What sawest thou, that thou hast done this thing? And Abraham said, Because I thought, Surely the fear of God is not in this place; and they will slay me for my wife's sake. And yet indeed she is my sister; she is the daughter of my father, but not the daughter of my mother; and she became my wife. And it came to pass, when God caused me to wander from my father's house, that I said unto her, This is thy kindness which thou shalt shew unto me; at every place whither we shall come, say of me, He is my brother. And Abimelech took sheep, and oxen, and manservants, and womenservants, and gave them unto Abraham, and restored him Sarah his wife. And Abimelech said, Behold, my land is before thee: dwell where it pleaseth thee. And unto Sarah he said, Behold, I have given thy brother a thousand pieces of silver: behold, he is to thee a covering of the eyes, unto all that are with thee, and with all other: thus she was reproved. So Abraham prayed unto God: and God healed Abimelech, and his wife, and his maidservants; and they bare children. For the Lord had fast closed up all the wombs of the house of Abimelech, because of Sarah Abraham's wife" (Genesis 20:1-18).

As Abraham's feet kept moving, his faith in and love for God kept growing. By learning, growing, and living, God brought Abraham to the spiritual plateau of Mount Moriah. It was at Mount Moriah, a pinnacle of sacrifice and surrender, that Abraham learned that God was Jehovah-Jireh. It was here at this place of testing, terror, and temptation that Abraham discovered that God has many ways to provide "A ram in the bush." At Moriah he learned that obedience to God's Word always results in victory over the terrors and trials of this life. God's request that Abraham offer up his son Isaac was unreasonable but faith in God delivers when we are asked to bear the unbearable.

If you can do something in your own strength you will never know what close fellowship with God can do. There once was a man who prayed to God for more faith. God surveyed his plans and replied, "You don't need any more faith than what you have in order to do what you plan to do." Big plans require great faith. Heavy loads require greater strength. God uses unbearable and unreasonable things to stretch us and build us up to the point that He wants to show us off. God never shows off that which He knows will never measure up. God never wastes our sufferings. In the midst of his trials, Job said,

"He knoweth the way that I take:/when he hath tested me, I shall come forth as gold" (Job 23:10).

God knows the road you travel. He also knows far more than you know what you need most.

A.   Sometimes your faith needs to be purified.

"Wherein ye greatly rejoice, though now for a reason, if need be, ye are in heaviness through manifold temptations: That the trial of your faith, being much more precious than of gold that perisheth, though it be tried with fire, might be found unto praise and honour and glory at the appearing of Jesus Christ: Whom having not seen, ye love; in whom, though now ye see him not, yet believing, ye rejoice with joy unspeakable and full of glory: Receiving the end of your faith, even the salvation of your souls" (1 Peter 1:6-9).

B.   Sometimes your faith needs to be matured.

"James, a servant of God and of the Lord Jesus Christ, to the twelve tribes which are scattered abroad, greeting. My brethren, count it all joy when ye fall into divers temptations; Knowing this, that the trying of your faith worketh patience. But let patience have her perfect work, that ye may be perfect and entire, wanting nothing. If any of you lack wisdom, let him ask of God, that giveth to all men liberally, and upbraideth not; and it shall be given him. But let him ask in faith, nothing wavering. For he that wavereth is like a wave of the sea driven with the wind and tossed" (James 1:1-6).

If you stay in God's will, you'll always be in the right place to see God work.

God told Abraham to go to Mount Moriah. Abraham obeyed. He carried Isaac, a knife, and a torch. Isaac was supposed to die. I find it remarkable that Abraham took what he needed to slay his son but he didn't take a shovel to bury him. Abraham told the two servants who went as far as they could go "I and the lad will go yonder and come again" (Genesis 22:5). He didn't know how God would do it, but he had lived long enough to trust God with the life of the son he loved.

Here's the good news. God did not fail Abraham and God will not fail you. It doesn't matter if it's cancer in your body or sorrow in your success. God never fails. When God defends you it really doesn't matter who attacks you. When life tries you—depend on God's provision. When people disappoint you—depend on the God who is always dependable, even if He asks you to do the unreasonable and bear the unbearable.

Ready to do God's bidding, Abraham's hand was stayed and the slaughter of his son was suspended by the sure sound of God's voice . . . God spared Isaac. God spared Isaac on Mount Moriah but He did not spare Jesus on Mount Calvary. On Mount Moriah God released Isaac from the bond of death but on Mount Calvary He suffered Jesus to die as the eternal Ram in the bush for all our sins. Because God did not hold Jesus back from the cross, you can be sure that He will never hold back anything that is in your best interest. The fact that God raised Jesus up as a root out of dry ground reveals His almightiness in ways that move angels to cheer.

"For he shall grow up before him as a tender plant, and as a root out of a dry ground: he hath no form nor comeliness; and when we shall see him, there is no beauty that we should desire him" (Isaiah 53:2).

The nature of growth is in accordance with the quality of the soil, but Jesus grew up as a root out of dry ground. There was nothing in the soil out of which Jesus came to account for His miraculous life. Consider His family. Mary and Joseph were simple people. They did not live in Jerusalem but in Nazareth. Upon Jesus' return to Nazareth scores of neighbors were astonished, asking, "Whence hath this man this wisdom and these mighty works?" They went on to expound upon their astonishment by asking "Is not this the carpenter's son? is not his mother called Mary? And his brethren; James and Joses, and Simon, and Judas? And his sisters, are they not all with us? Whence then hath this man all these things?" (Matthew 13:54-56). There was nothing in our Lord's family to account for His greatness. The only explanation for our Lord's passion, power, and possession is the God factor. His family had no money to send Him to Jerusalem to sit at the famous feet of Gamaliel, the scholar who taught Saul of Tarsus. The only explanation for our Lord's deeds of power and unmatched holiness rests in God alone. It was all He had and it was all He needed. When you get to a point in your life where you find that God is all that you have, you will find that God is all that you need.

This world can be a dangerous place, but because there is a safe dwelling place in victory, every day is already secured. If you abide in the Lord and love Him with all your heart, soul, and mind, your faith in God's protection can carry you through all dangers and every fear you face. Give God your fears and He will give you more faith. Be as honest with Him as was the weary father who said with tears, "Lord I believe; help thou my unbelief" (Mark 9:24). If you will be honest He will be faithful. If you will trust Him He will surround you with His protection, peace, and prosperity. The outcome of the war between good and evil will be apparent if you learn to acknowledge God as Jehovah-Jireh. God has already provided for you the answers you need to live victoriously in His written, invincible, and inerrant Word.

If you have lost your faith you don't have to borrow the faith of others. You can't live between the cradle and the grave off borrowed faith. If doubts trouble you, take them to God and have it out with your doubts. If you will stay in the Word of God you will get a new vision of light and it will summon new strength to your feeble faith.

An old sign painter, was approaching retirement, so he took an apprentice up a steep roof to paint a sign. He pushed a short ladder out of the window and said to the young man, "You get out on the ladder and I will pass to you the necessary materials." The young man looked at the ladder, and with his eyes he measured the depth to the earth, and with shattered nerves, he drew back, and said, "I can't do it, it is too dangerous; life is too sweet and the risk is too great." The old painter said, "Young man there is nothing to fear, for the ladder has sharp prongs on the underside, and when you put your weight on it, it digs deep down into the roof. Just try it." The lad stepped cautiously out of the window, and felt the spikes dig into the shingles, and then stood upon it with his full weight and painted a magnificent sign.

That's something we all need to do—try our faith in the provisions that Jehovah-Jireh has made.

(1) Try your Faith in God's provisions and He will honor your faith.

"He that dwelleth in the secret place of the most High shall abide under the shadow of the Almighty. I will say of the Lord, He is my refuge and my fortress: my God; in him will I trust. Surely he shall deliver thee from the snare of the fowler, and from the noisome pestilence. He shall cover thee with his feathers, and under his wings shalt thou trust: his truth shall be thy shield and buckler. Thou shalt not be afraid for the terror by night; nor for the arrow that flieth by day; nor for the pestilence that walketh in darkness; nor for the destruction that wasteth at noonday. A thousand shall fall at thy side, and ten thousand at thy right hand; but it shall not come nigh thee. Only with thine eyes shalt thou behold and see the reward of the wicked. Because thou hast made the Lord, which is my refuge, even the most High, thy habitation; there shall no evil befall thee, neither shall any plague come nigh thy dwelling. For he shall give his angels charge over thee, to keep thee in all thy ways. They shall bear thee up in their hands, lest thou dash thy foot against a stone. Thou shalt tread upon the lion and adder: the young lion and the dragon shalt thou trample under feet. Because he hath set his love upon me, therefore will I deliver him: I will set him on high, because he hath known my name. He shall call upon me, and I will answer him: I will be with him in trouble, I will deliver him, and honour him. With long life will I satisfy him, and shew him my salvation" (Psalm 91).

A. The Lord will provide protection.

I once read a simple statement on the wall of a Montgomery, Alabama, service station. It read "If you need a penny take one. If you need two pennies take two. If you need three pennies get a job." How often have we seen a flyer on the wall of some secretaries' cubicle that says "I can only please one person a day, and today ain't your day. (By the way tomorrow ain't looking too good either.)" These truths appear comical to us, but how humorous are they? How blessed we are that we serve a God who never tires of meeting his children's needs. Jehovah-Jireh is an everyday Provider who prepares new mercies each new morning. God provides protection in this war between good and evil by many means.

In Psalm 91:

A. He protects us by providing secret shelter—Verse 1 & 2

B. By covering with his wings—Verse 4

C. He protects us as the "Most High" God—no danger can touch him.

D. He protects us as "God Jehovah"—no danger can outlast him.

God protects us from all kinds of dangers; secret, hidden, open, obvious, natural, supernatural, and overwhelming. He protects us at all times. Dangers, hidden or obvious, all meet their defeat and destruction in the protective providence of Jehovah-Jireh.

B. The Lord will provide a table that is spread.

That "Prince of Preachers," Dr. Sandy Ray, who now lives with God, shared with me a wonderful story when I was a young preacher. Dr. Ray spoke to me about a man from Europe who had spent most of his life saving enough money to purchase his passage on a ship headed for the United States. He bought his ticket. After that purchase He had only a few dollars left for clothing and food so he decided to buy a box of cheese and crackers to eat during his passage. While other passengers ate wonderfully prepared meals this man stole away to his secret daily date with his cheese and crackers. He crossed an ocean with his meager diet until the last day of the trip. A man and his wife happened up on the man as he ate his cheese and crackers in his self-imposed state of isolation. They questioned him why he was eating alone, and asked him to join them in the dining room. He explained that he only had enough money to buy his ticket and had nothing left to pay for a meal. They remarked to him, "Sir did you know the cost for the meals were paid when you bought your ticket?"

God has a lot of good and faithful soldiers on the battlefield who don't know that God has reserved a place at the table for them. Too many of God's people are fainting along the way from a cheese and cracker diet while the Almighty has spread a banquet table of good things for them before they get to heaven. Child of God, you are in a fight, but you are in the army of the King who has paid for all your supplies. Paul reminded us that "No soldier going to war bears his own expense." God has provided a place for you at his table. Try him! Trust Him! Test Him! Your needs have already been paid for. Take Him at His Word! Miracles and supernatural intervention is available, accessible, and assured. Even when danger and judgement come to others, remember Psalm 91:7-8: "A thousand shall fall at thy side, and ten thousand at thy right hand; but it shall not come nigh thee. Only with thine eyes shalt thou behold and see the reward of the wicked."

God has fashioned us for faith and not fear. Those who live in an ongoing state of fear become a liability to God's cause and their own good. Many find that their universe continually falls to pieces when they are self-centered rather than God-centered. Self-centered attitudes give birth to fear. When people change the center of their lives from self to God all of their sums come out right; but as long as the center is wrong, nothing will really come out right.

On the road that leads to glory, the God we work for is the God we work with. In a time of war, it's good to have the presence of the one who cannot lose and will never die. And now Lord I thank you that you are Jehovah-Jireh, pronounce it, say it, remember it, and live with it daily.

Chapter 9

PRAYER

I. Facing the Terrorist of Physical Sickness

Heavenly Father, I acknowledge that You desire my prosperity in physical health as well as spiritual health. I claim, at this point, no power in my own strength but all power through Your strength. I am in Your hands. I am Yours from the crown of my head to the soles of my feet. Every nerve, cell, artery, vein, muscle and bone in this body which is Your temple is in Your hands. I seek Your healing in Your way according to Your schedule. I bless You Father for the healing gift of Jesus Christ—my Lord. I come to You with Your own words. Thankful that, "he was wounded for our transgressions, he was bruised for our iniquities: the chastisement of our peace was upon him; and with his stripes we are healed." (Isaiah 53:5)

"Heal me, O Lord, and I shall be healed; save me, and I shall be saved: for thou art my praise (Jeremiah 17:14).

I can face anything now because I know I am not alone. I may be sick, but I thank You that I am not alone. The Good News that You have given me overwhelms any other news I might receive. My illness only reminds me that I am getting closer and closer to You and all terror loses its power as I think of finally seeing Your blessed face. You and I have come to this hour and I thank You that I know that You and I will come through this hour together. There have been times I have failed You but, there has never been a moment when You have failed me. Any surgery I may have or have had pales when I think of the nail prints You still wear from standing in my place at Calvary. Father, I am forever touched by Your loving and tender care. I come to You with my need for healing and restoration, and I reach out to take all that You desire I should have. I know that You and only You can make things right. I accept Your wisdom and I claim victory over this terrorist of pain. I bind, in the name of Jesus Christ, every enemy of my physical health. I give You thanks this day for the healing touch of our Lord, which has brought wholeness to diseased and broken lives and restored to all of us who love You a healing that is to be echoed all over our world. I thank You that there is no defeat in me because there is no defeat in You. In the name of Jesus I pray. Amen.

II. Facing the Terrorist of Financial Trouble

God, who counts His cattle by the hill rather than by the head, in Your word You said, "For every beast of the forest is mine, and the cattle upon a thousand hills" (Psalm 50:10). Father, You said, "If I were hungry, I would not tell thee: for the world is mine and the fullness thereof" (Psalm 50:12). Father, You said, "call upon me in the day of trouble: I will deliver thee, and thou shalt glorify me" (Psalm 50:15). Father, You said, "I will rebuke the devourer for your sakes, and he shall not destroy the fruits of your ground; neither shall your vine cast her fruit before the time in the field, saith the Lord of hosts" (Malachi 3:11).

I bring to You, O God, my fear of being in want, of not having enough, of running out of money before I run out of month, of needing today what is not supposed to come until tomorrow, of facing an outgo that is greater than my income, of looking at today's payment that is due with nothing more than a promise. And yet, the promise I cling to is one that removes me from the land of not enough to the land of more than enough. I cling to the promise that I have because it is a promise that comes from You. I believe that You will supply all my needs according to Your riches in glory by Christ Jesus (Philippians 4:19). This hope that I have is not in my wealth or works but is in the restored covenant of Jesus Christ our Lord. This hope that I have will send me from this prayer back into the face of my financial challenges knowing that You will meet my every need. Like Hezekiah the King who took the threatening letter from his enemy and "went up into the house of the Lord, and spread it before the Lord (2 Kings 19:14), I spread this bill, this document, this summons, this threat regardless of where it comes, from before You. My name may be on it but this battle is the Lord's. My address might be on it but this matter belongs to You. I can't think my way out. I can't work my way out. I can't fight my way out, so, as I lay this need before You I do so trusting in Your power and Your power alone. I trust in You, Father with all my heart; and I lean not to my own understanding (Proverbs 3:5). My confidence is in thy unfailing bounty and I know that You will never place more one me than I can bear. This is a critical time. I will not minimize the threat. But, at the same time I will not give in or give up. I know that the rainbow will come because You will not allow any storm to last forever. It is, O Lord, beneath Your eyes that every heart trembles. Keep me Father steady in my walk with You, constant in my devotion and always obedient in Your service. In the matchless name of the Lamb of God—Jesus—who takes away all sin, I pray. Amen.

III. FACING THE TERRORIST WHO STEALS OUR PEACE

Father in heaven, I know I belong to You and that this world has a hostile reception for me. I have resolved, by Your grace and Your mercy, to simply receive Your peace. I know that You will keep me in perfect peace, as long as my mind is focused on thee (Isaiah 26:3). Innumerable barriers lie in the way to steal my peace of mind; yet in spite of depravity and ongoing obstructions, I will, "Be careful for nothing; but in everything by prayer and supplication with thanksgiving let my requests be made known to you. And the peace of God, which passeth all understanding, shall keep [my] heart and my mind through Christ Jesus (Philippians 4:6-7).

As I face this terrorist that would steal my peace, I pray that You will accept what I offer in Christian love to Jesus Christ our Lord. I give only that which is already Yours. Through Jesus, with Jesus, in Jesus, lives all I have to give that is worth giving. But Father as I give to You, I cannot help but place before You all my broken dreams and broken days. I give to You my battered will and my bruised body. I give to You my confused mind and my unraveled spirit. I kneel before You with a broken spirit because I know what I have been. Yet I come boldly, searching for the eyes of Jesus so that I can see what I will become. In the face of so much confusion I know that there is one thing that I can always count on: You are faithful. Jesus is steadfast and Your Holy Spirit will see me safely to Your holy bosom.

I know that the strength of faith is expressed in the victories that it will achieve in spite of the problems that are involved. I know that discouragement takes its toll on multitudes everyday. I pray I will "stagger not at the promise of God through unbelief; but [live my life] strong in faith, giving glory to God" (Romans 4:20). Long ago Paul said even though the spirit is willing the flesh is weak." I agree and I come before You to relinquish my memories so that they might be drained of all of their bitterness. I will not balk, hesitate, vacillate, or stagger at Your promises. You have been eyes to the blind, ears for the deaf and feet for the lame. You have not forsaken me even for one quick moment. You have surrounded me with everlasting mercies and those mercies have made me stronger and given me both peace with You and peace from You. I praise thee and ask these blessings in the name of our Christ. Amen.

IV. Facing the Terrorist Threatening our Nation

Almighty God, You defeated Adolf Hitler in Germany with a snowflake on the Russian front. You defeated Joseph Stalin in Russia and have made the Soviet Union into nothing more than a memory. You took a baby's tear, a daughter's heart, and a shepherd's rod and turned Pharaoh and his entire army into food for the fish of the Red Sea. You took one angel and destroyed one hundred and eighty-five thousand Assyrian troops in one night (2 Kings 19). Father God, only You could have fed Your people until Your angel went to work. Only an Almighty God could say to Your people, "And this shall be a sign unto thee, ye shall eat this year such things as grow of themselves, and in the second year that which springeth of the same; and in the third year sow ye, and reap, and plant vineyards, and eat the fruits thereof" (2 Kings 19:29).

Father God You took Gideon, three hundred men, and some trumpets and pitchers and put the entire Midianite Army to flight (Judges 7).

Osama bin Laden has hurt us as a nation. What happened to some of us on September 11, 2001, could have happened to any of us. Thank You for keeping our enemies from doing all that they desired to do. Thank You for holding family members together who never had a chance to say goodbye to loved ones that departed. We know that it was Your amazing grace that kept us and is keeping us day by day. We rise with strength knowing that You hold our lives and our national future in Your hands. We bless You for shining Your light of love in our hearts and we go forth as a nation to startle the world with the neverending confidence of hope, generosity, and love.

The fates of Hitler, Stalin, Pharaoh, Sennacherib, and the Midianite army remind us that Osama bin Laden, Al Qaida, and every suicide bomber's days are set and positioned for judgment.

We pray for these enemies because You told us to do so. We ask that they will come to a place of repentance. It is You, the God of all glory, that made this world and brought beauty out of chaos. Guard, guide, console, and sustain us to do Your work to make this world a better place for all of Your children. Grant unto us as a nation that faith that will remain a lamp unto our weary feet and a light unto our meandering path. Thy law to us is liberty and the real cry of our hearts is that we will become "one nation under God."

Enable us, O Lord, to look upon those who are dying and tell them that death is overthrown. Help us in this battle of good and evil to see that You are writing the story of the Resurrection upon the face of this whole world. We will face each day with our sense of being led by You and therefore we will never become victims of circumstance. We will recommit ourselves to be actors and not reactors. We will work from the principles You have taught us and not from the pressures of this fleeting hour in history. We thank You that You are with us in all of our struggles, and one day the kingdoms of this world will become the kingdoms of our Christ and He shall reign forever and ever. Hallelujah! In Jesus' name we pray. Amen.

V. Facing the Terrorist of Guilt

You amaze me, Heavenly Father, with the greatness of Your unbounded love for me. In the midst of my imperfect life, You have given me the gift of Jesus Christ. You are my righteousness. I have heard the voice of Jesus charging me to go forth, and yet there have been times when my heart was not in Your call to evangelize to the lost. I know that You have called me to bear up others, to pray for others and to be open to the movement of Your Holy Spirit. I have failed and satanic forces seek to dress me in a cloak of guilt. I have failed and the demons of selective memory seek to tempt me to believe that my sins are greater than Your grace. I have left undone far too much and I have said, done, and felt the viper of sin in my own heart. And yet, as I come, I have no fear because I come to You, Father, with what You have said to sinners like me. I come to You in the name of Jesus. I come because You said: "There is therefore now no condemnation to them which are in Christ Jesus, who walk not after the flesh, but after the Spirit" (Romans 8:1).

I have felt helpless at times but I bless You that I know that I am not hopeless, because you said: "For God sent not his Son into the world to condemn the world; but that the world through him might be saved. He that believeth in him is not condemned: but he that believeth not is condemned already, because he hath not believed in the name of the only begotten Son of God" (John 3:17-18).

I, like other sheep, have in my past times gone astray but Father, You know that I have repented and because of my repentance and Your mercy I rejoice in saying:

"He hath not dealt with us after our sins; nor rewarded us according to our iniquities. As far as the east is from the west, so far hath he removed our transgression from us" (Psalm 103:10, 12).

I bring to You my vulnerabilities because I know I am bringing them to the One True God who has the power to overcome all. I give to You all of my sins. I come to You to be renewed and recharged. Please teach me how to take in your power, lay hold of Your resources, and align my heart with Your purposes. I hear You saying: "For I will be merciful to their unrighteousness, and their sins and their iniquities will I remember no more" (Hebrews 8:12).

I hear You saying: "Therefore if any man be in Christ, he is a new creature; old things are passed away; behold, all things are become new" (2 Corinthians 5:17). I hear You saying: "I, even I, am he that blotteth out thy transgressions for mine own sake, and will not remember thy sins" (Isaiah 43:25). I hear You saying: "Verily, verily, I say unto you, He that heareth my word, and believeth in him that sent me, hath everlasting life, and shall not come into condemnation; but is passed from death unto life" (John 5:24).

I hear You saying: "If we confess our sins, he is faithful and just to forgive us our sins, and to cleanse us from all unrighteousness" (1 John 1:9). "Blessed is he whose transgression is forgiven, whose sin is covered" (Psalm 32:1).

I turn to You because I hear You saying:

"For if ye turn again unto the Lord, your brethren and your children shall find compassion before them that lead them captive, so that they shall come again into this land: for the Lord your God is gracious and merciful, and will not turn away his face from you, if ye return unto him" (2 Chronicles 30:9).

I know that You will not honor frivolous curiosity. I know that some shut You out and You never knock again. I know that some turn from You and You refuse to plead with them. I open my heart. I repent not simply with my tears but with my life. I lay my guilt before Calvary because it is too heavy a load for these shoulders of mine. And now I pray, let the words of my mouth and the meditation of my heart and the direction of my life be acceptable in thy sight. Amen.

VI. FACING THE TERRORIST SPIRIT OF THE ANTICHRIST

Heavenly Father, in Your inerrant and invincible Word You have warned us through the Apostle John by saying "Little children, it is the last time: and as ye have heard that antichrist shall come, even now are there many antichrists; whereby we know that it is the last time" (1 John 2:18). I know that the spirit of the antichrist is behind false reports, false doctrines, false saviors, and false finishing lines. I sense the spirit is not only against Christ but is busy trying to substitute counterfeits for the real thing that is found in Jesus and Jesus alone. I thank thee, Father, that I know that when people are wrong about Jesus, they are wrong about you, because Jesus is Your final and complete revelation to us.

Some have been deceived but Your Spirit in me has shown me evil for what it is. I see evil dressed in a shepherd's wardrobe. I see the lying wonders as the masses move toward the slaughter. I know that what I witness is not the work of an originator but the plan of an imitator. In this day when some think they are living large, I sense the need to prove myself to be a power and not a farce. The clouds that hang over us are dark and ominous as we see mothers selling their babies for a fix and fathers trading their souls for a success that will never come. We are in a war that our generation cannot afford to lose. The social perils are thick. The enemy is powerful. Atheists are defiant. Agnostics are aggressive. Some that are into Jesus have no desire to have Jesus in them.

Some who want to march with the army have no desire to be anything more than an audience. The road is long. The struggle is on. The fight is fierce. The hills are high but my faith in you strengthens me and empowers me with a burning message for the fallen and the fearful. The battle need not be lost. The children need not perish. The families need not fall apart for thou art full of compassion and lovingkindness. You have given us sharp glances of your Love and we feel the presence of Your faithfulness. Thank You Father for binding us with cords that cannot be broken by human strength. Thank You Father for giving us a freedom that cannot be measured by human imagination. Thank You, Father that it doesn't matter whether we are very young or very old, very strong or very weak, we come to You as sheep of Your fold, trusting in your guidance and resting in Your victory. In the name of Jesus we pray. Amen.

VII. Facing the Terrorist of of Discouragement

Almighty God, You know that we are often an impatient nation of people. You have given us so much so quickly that we become discouraged when the victory doesn't come immediately. Forgive us for our failures due to our impatience. You have already spoken to our hearts as You said, "Let not your heart be troubled: ye believe in God, believe also in me" (John 14:1). Help us to not be ashamed to be dependent upon You and upon one another. Give us, God the blessed insight to greet each battle with a salvation and a song. In this delicate and sometimes difficult job of working together, teach us all to simply take one day at a time. We thank You that not only do we have work to do but You have given and you will give us the strength to do our work in Your way and in Your time. Look tenderly, Father upon our leaders and all of Your soldiers.

You have provided us with the formula for conquest. You have bought us. You have taught us and You have gone before us as a guiding light reminding us to "seek ye first the kingdom of God, and his righteousness; and all these things shall be added unto you. Take therefore no thought for the morrow: for the morrow shall take thought for the things of itself. Sufficient unto the day is the evil thereof" (Matthew 6:33-34).

Heal our discouraged hearts by reminding us that every minute is fragile and every hour can be holy. In our hurried pace we have sought to hurry You. Forgive us and breathe on us so that we might take a new look at everything that is of eternal significance. You have shown us Your love with the cross and You have revealed Your power through the resurrection of our Lord and Savior Jesus Christ. Help us to see ourselves through the eyes of Your dear Son. We know that the lonely can find companionship and the oppressed can come to know themselves as members of the body of Christ. Because this is so, we will overcome every demon of depression and discouragement. We rise up with the words that You have given us in Your Word: "We are troubled on every side, yet not distressed; we are perplexed, but not in despair; Persecuted, but not forsaken; cast down, but not destroyed" (2 Corinthians 4:8-9).

Thank You, O God, for showing us the way back from the pit of discouragement and giving us the coverage to take it. We affirm to You that we shall let no man or spirit steal our faith, poison our trust, or cloud our judgement. In the name of our Christ we pray. Amen.

Chapter 10

Wars, Weapons, and Warriors

(1) Exodus 17:8-16—**The value of prayer while waging the war on terror:** *"Then came Amalek, and fought with Israel in Rephidim. And Moses said unto Joshua, Choose us out men, and go out, fight with Amalek: tomorrow I will stand on the top of the hill with the rod of God in mine hand. So Joshua did as Moses had said to him, and fought with Amalek: and Moses, Aaron, and Hur went up to the top of the hill. And it came to pass, when Moses held up his hand, that Israel prevailed: and when he let down his hand, Amalek prevailed. But Moses' hands were heavy; and they took a stone, and put it under him and he sat thereon; and Aaron and Hur stayed up his hands, the one on the one side, and the other on the other side; and his hands were steady until the going down of the sun. And Joshua discomfited Amalek and his people with the edge of the sword. And the Lord said unto Moses, Write this for a memorial in a book, and rehearse it in the ears of Joshua: for I will utterly put out the remembrance of Amalek from under heaven. And Moses built an altar, and called the name of it Jehovahnissi: For he said, Because the Lord hath sworn that the Lord will have war with Amalek from generation to generation.*

(2) Joshua 6:1-20—**Following God's orders: even if there is no crack in the wall—it will fall:** *"Now Jericho was straitly shut up because of the children of Israel: none went out, and none came in. And the Lord said unto Joshua, See, I have given into thine hand Jericho, and the king thereof, and the mighty men of valour. And ye shall compass the city, all ye men of war, and go round about the city once. Thus shalt thou*

do six days. And seven priests shall bear before the ark seven trumpets of ram's horns: and the seventh day ye shall compass the city seven times, and the priests shall blow with the trumpets. And it shall come to pass, that when they make a long blast with the ram's horn, and when ye hear the sound of the trumpet, all the people shall shout with a great shout; and the wall of the city shall fall down flat, and the people shall ascend up every man straight before him. And Joshua the son of Nun called the priests, and said unto them, Take up the ark of the covenant, and let seven priests bear seven trumpets of rams' horns before the ark of the Lord. And he said unto the people, Pass on, and compass the city, and let him that is armed pass on before the ark of the Lord. And it came to pass, when Joshua had spoken unto the people, that the seven priests bearing the seven trumpets of rams' horn passed on before the Lord, and blew with the trumpets: and the ark of the covenant of the Lord followed them. And the armed men went before the priests that blew with the trumpets, and the reward came after the ark, the priests going on, and blowing with the trumpets. And Joshua had commanded the people, saying, Ye shall not shout, nor make any noise with your voice, neither shall any word proceed out of your mouth, until the day I bid you shout; then shall ye shout. So the ark of the Lord compassed the city, going about it once: and they came into the camp, and lodged in the camp. And Joshua rose early in the morning, and the priests took up the ark of the Lord. And seven priests bearing seven trumpets of rams' horns before the ark of the Lord went on continually, and blew with the trumpets: and the armed men went before them; but the reward came after the ark of the Lord, the priests going on, and blowing with the trumpets. And the second day they compassed the city once, and returned into the camp: so they did six days. And it came to pass on the seventh day, that they rose early about the dawning of the day, and compassed the city after the same manner seven times: only on that day they compassed the city seven times. And it came to pass at the seventh time, when the priests blew with the trumpets, Joshua said unto the people, Shout; for the Lord hath given you the city. And the city shall be accursed, even it, and all that are therein, to the Lord: only Rahab the harlot shall live, she and all that are with her in the house, because she hid the messengers that we sent. And ye, in any wise keep yourselves from the accursed thing, lest ye make yourselves accursed, when ye take of the accursed thing, and make the camp of Israel a curse, and trouble it. But all the silver, and gold, and vessels of brass and iron, are consecrated unto the Lord: they shall come into the treasury of the Lord. So the people shouted when the priests blew with the trumpets: and it came to pass, when the people heard the sound of the trumpet, and the people shouted with a great shout, that the wall fell down flat, so that the people went up into the city, every man straight before him, and they took the city."

(3) Judges 7:1-23—**You can win the war even when the odds are against you:** *"Then Jerubbaal, who is Gideon, and all the people that were with him, rose up early, and pitched beside the well of Harod: so that the host of the Midianites were on the north side of them, by the hill of Moreh, in the valley. And the Lord said unto Gideon, The people that are with thee are too many for me to give the Midianites into their hands, lest Israel vaunt themselves against me, saying, Mine own hand hath saved me. Now therefore go to, proclaim in the ears of the people, saying, Whosoever is fearful and afraid, let him return and depart early from mount Gilead. And there returned of the people twenty and two thousand; and there remained ten thousand. And the Lord said unto Gideon, The people are yet too many; bring them down unto the water, and I will try them for thee there: and it shall be, that of whom I say unto thee, This shall go with thee, the same shall go with thee; and of whomsoever I say unto thee, This shall not go with thee, the same shall not go. So he brought down the people unto the water: and the Lord said unto Gideon, Every one that lappeth of the water with his tongue, as a dog lappeth, him shalt thou set by himself; likewise every one that boweth down upon his knees to drink. And the number of them that lapped, putting their hand to their mouth, were three hundred men: but all the rest of the people bowed down upon their knees to drink water. And the Lord said unto Gideon, By the three hundred men that lapped will I save you, and deliver the Midianites into thine hand: and let all the other people go every man unto his place. So the people took victuals in their hand, and their trumpets: and he sent all the rest of Israel every man unto his tent, and retained those three hundred men: and the host of Midian was beneath him in the valley. And it came to pass the same night, that the Lord said unto him, Arise, get thee down unto the host; for I have delivered it into thine hand. But if thou*

fear to go down, go thou with Phurah thy servant down to the host. And thou shalt hear what they say; and afterward shall thine hands be strengthened to do down unto the host. Then went he down with Phurah his servant outside of the armed men that were in the host. And the Midianites and the Amalekites and all the children of the east lay along in the valley like grasshoppers for multitude; and their camels were without number, as the sand by the sea side for multitude. And when Gideon was come, behold, there was a man that told a dream unto his fellow, and said, Behold, I dreamed a dream, and, lo, a cake of barley bread tumbled into the host of Midian, and came unto a tent, and smote it that it fell, and overturned it, that the tent lay along. And his fellow answered and said, This is nothing else save the sword of Gideon the son of Joash, a man of Israel: for into his hand hath God delivered Midian, and all the host. And it was so, when Gideon heard the telling of the dream, and the interpretation thereof, that he worshipped, and returned into the host of Israel, and said, Arise; for the Lord hath delivered into your hand the host of Midian. And he divided the three hundred men into three companies, and he put a trumpet in every man's hand, with empty pitchers, and lamps within the pitchers. And he said unto them, Look on me, and do likewise: and, behold, when I come to the outside of the camp, it shall be that, as I do, so shall ye do. When I blow with a trumpet, I and all that are with me, then blow ye the trumpets also on every side of all the camp, and say, The sword of the Lord and of Gideon. So Gideon, and the hundred men that were with him, came unto the outside of the camp in the beginning of the middle watch; and they had but newly set the watch: and they blew the trumpets, and brake the pitchers that were in their hands. And the three companies blew the trumpets, and brake the pitchers, and held the lamps in their left hands, and the trumpets in their right hand to blow withal: and they cried, The sword of the Lord, and of Gideon. And they stood every man in his place round about the camp: and all the host ran, and cried, and fled. And the three hundred blew the trumpets, and the Lord set every man's sword against his fellow, even throughout all the host: and the host fled to Bethshittah in Zererath, and to the border of Abelmeholah, unto Tabbath. And the men of Israel gathered themselves together out of Naphtali, and out of Asher, and out of all Manasseh, and pursued after the Midianites."

(4) 1 Samuel 17:32-51—**The battle is the Lord's**: *"And David said to Saul, Let no man's heart fail because of him; thy servant will go and fight with this Philistine. And Saul said to David, Thou art not able to go against this Philistine to fight with him: for thou are but a youth, and he a man of war from his youth. And David said unto Saul, Thy servant kept his father's sheep, and there came a lion, and a bear, and took a lamb out of the flock: And I went out after him, and smote him, and delivered it out of his mouth: and when he arose against me, I caught him by his beard, and smote him, and slew him. Thy servant slew both the lion and the bear: and this uncircumcised Philistine shall be as one of them, seeing he hath defied the armies of the living God. David said moreover, The Lord that delivered me out of the paw of the lion, and out of the paw of the bear, he will deliver me out of the hand of this Philistine. And Saul said unto David, Go, and the Lord be with thee. And Saul armed David with his armour, and he put an helmet of brass upon his head; also he armed him with a coat of mail. And David girded his sword upon his armour, and he assayed to go; for he had not proved it. And David said unto Saul, I cannot go with these; for I have not proved them. And David put them off him. And he took his staff in his hand, and chose him five smooth stones out of the brook, and put them in a shepherd's bag which he had, even in a scrip; and his sling was in his hand: and he drew near to the Philistine. And the Philistine came on and drew near unto David; and the man that bare the shield went before him. And when the Philistine looked about, and saw David, he disdained him: for he was but a youth, and ruddy, and of a fair countenance. And the Philistine said unto David, Am I a dog, that thou comest to me with staves? And the Philistine cursed David by his gods. And the Philistine said to David, Come to me, and I will give thy flesh unto the fowls of the air, and to the beasts of the field. Then said David to the Philistine, Thou comest to me with a sword, and with a spear, and with a shield: but I come to thee in the name of the Lord of hosts, the God of the armies of Israel, whom thou hast defied. This day will the Lord deliver thee into mine hand; and I will smite thee, and take thine head from thee; and I will give the carcasses of the host of the Philistines this day unto the fowls of the air, and the wild beasts of the earth; that all the earth may know that there is a God in Israel. And all this assembly shall know that the Lord saveth not with*

sword and spear: for the battle is the Lord's, and he will give you into our hands. And it came to pass, when the Philistine arose, and came, and drew nigh to meet David, that David hastened, and ran toward the army to meet the Philistine. And David put his hand in his bag, and took hence a stone, and slang it, and smote the Philistine in his forehead, that the stone sunk into his forehead; and he fell upon his face to the earth. So David prevailed over the Philistine with a sling and with a stone, and smote the Philistine and slew him; but there was no sword in the hand of David. So David ran, and stood upon the Philistine, and took his sword, and drew it out of the sheath thereof, and slew him, and cut off his head therewith. And when the Philistines saw their champion was dead, they fled."

(5) 2 Chronicles 20:1-30—**The war won by singing songs and giving praise:** *"It came to pass after this also, that the children of Moab, and the children of Ammon, and with them other beside the Ammonites, came against Jehoshaphat to battle. Then there came some that told Jehoshaphat, saying, There cometh a great multitude against thee from beyond the sea on this side Syria; and, behold, they be in Hazazontamar, which is Engedi. And Jehoshaphat feared, and set himself to seek the Lord, and proclaimed a fast throughout all Judah. And Judah gathered themselves together, to ask help of the Lord: even out of all the cities of Judah they came to seek the Lord. And Jehoshaphat stood in the congregation of Judah and Jerusalem, in the house of the Lord, before the new court, And said, O Lord God of our fathers, art not thou God in heaven? and rulest not thou over all the kingdoms of the heathen? and in thine hand is there not power and might, so that none is able to withstand thee? Art not thou our God, who didst drive out the inhabitants of this land before thy people Israel, and gavest it to the seed of Abraham thy friend for ever? And they dwelt therein, and have built thee a sanctuary therein for thy name saying, If, when evil cometh upon us, as the sword, judgment, or pestilence, or famine, we stand before this house, and in thy presence, (for thy name is in this house,) and cry unto thee in our affliction, then thou wilt hear and help. And now, behold, the children of Ammon and Moab and mount Seir, whom thou wouldest not let Israel invade, when they came out of the land of Egypt, but they turned from them, and destroyed them*

not; Behold, I say, how they reward us, to come to cast us out of thy possession, which thou hast given us to inherit. O our God, wilt thou not judge them? for we have no might against this great company that cometh against us; neither know we what to do: but our eyes are upon thee. And all Judah stood before the Lord, with their little ones, their wives, and their children. Then upon Jahaziel the son of Zechariah, the son of Benaiah, the son of Jeiel, the son of Mattaniah, a Levite of the sons of Asaph, came the Spirit of the Lord in the midst of the congregation; And he said, Hearken ye, all Judah, and ye inhabitants of Jerusalem, and thou king Jehoshaphat, Thus saith the Lord unto you, Be not afraid nor dismayed by reason of this great multitude; for the battle is not yours, but God's. Tomorrow go ye down against them: behold, they come up by the cliff of Ziz; and ye shall find them at the end of the brook, before the wilderness of Jeruel. Ye shall not need to fight in this battle: set yourselves, stand ye still, and see the salvation of the Lord with you, O Judah and Jerusalem: fear not, nor be dismayed; tomorrow go out against them: for the Lord will be with you. And Jehoshaphat bowed his head with his face to the ground: and all Judah and the inhabitants of Jerusalem fell before the Lord, worshipping the Lord. And the Levites, of the children of the Kohathites, and of the children of the Korhites, stood up to praise the Lord God of Israel with a loud voice on high. And they rose early in the morning, and went forth into the wilderness of Tekoa: and as they went forth, Jehoshaphat stood and said, Hear me, O Judah, and ye inhabitants of Jerusalem; Believe in the Lord your God, so shall ye be established; believe his prophets, so shall ye prosper. And when he had consulted with the people, he appointed singers unto the Lord, and that should praise the beauty of holiness, as they went out before the army, and to say, Praise the Lord; for his mercy endureth for ever. And when they began to sing and to praise, the Lord set ambushments against the children of Ammon, Moab, and mount Seir, which were come against Judah; and they were smitten. For the children of Ammon and Moab stood up against the inhabitants of mount Seir, utterly to slay and destroy them: and when they had made an end of the inhabitants of Seir, every one helped to destroy another. And when Judah came toward the watch tower in the wilderness, they looked unto the multitude, and, behold, they were dead bodies fallen to the earth, and none escaped. And when Jehoshaphat and his people came to take *away the spoil of them, they found among them in abundance both riches with the dead bodies, and precious jewels, which they stripped off for themselves, more than they could carry away: and they were three days in gathering of the spoil, it was so much. And on the fourth day they assembled themselves in the valley of Berachah; for there they blessed the Lord: therefore the name of the same place was called, The valley of Berachah, unto this day. Then they returned, every man of Judah and Jerusalem, and Jehoshaphat in the forefront of them, to go again to Jerusalem with joy; for the Lord had made them to rejoice over their enemies. And they came to Jerusalem with psalteries and harps and trumpets unto the house of the Lord. And the fear of God was on all the kingdoms of those countries, when they had heard that the Lord fought against the enemies of Israel. So the realm of Jehoshaphat was quiet: for his God gave him rest round about."*

(6) Psalm 37—**A blessing to take to every battle against terror:** *"Fret not thyself because of evildoers, neither be thou envious against the workers of iniquity. For they shall soon be cut down like the grass, and wither as the green herb. Trust in the Lord, and do good; so shalt thou dwell in the land, and verily thou shalt be fed. Delight thyself also in the Lord:/and he shall give thee the desires of thine heart. Commit thy way unto the Lord; trust also in him; and he shall bring it to pass. And he shall bring forth thy righteousness as the light, and thy judgment as the noonday. Rest in the Lord, and wait patiently for him: fret not thyself because of him who prospereth in his way, because of the man who bringeth wicked devices to pass. Cease from anger, and forsake wrath: fret not thyself in any wise to do evil. For evildoers shall be cut off: but those that wait upon the Lord, they shall inherit the earth. For yet a little while, and the wicked shall not be: yea, thou shalt diligently consider his place, and it shall not be. But the meek shall inherit the earth; and shall delight themselves in the abundance of peace. The wicked plotteth against the just, and gnasheth upon him with his teeth. The Lord shall laugh at him: for he seeth that his day is coming. The wicked have drawn out the sword, and have bent their bow, to cast down the poor and needy, and to slay such as be of upright conversation. Their sword shall enter into their own heart, and their bows shall be broken. A little that a righteous man hath is bet-*

ter than the riches of many wicked. For the arms of the wicked shall be broken: but the Lord upholdeth the righteous. The Lord knoweth the days of the upright: and their inheritance shall be for ever. They shall not be ashamed in the evil time: and in the days of famine they shall be satisfied. But the wicked shall perish, and the enemies of the Lord shall be as the fat of lambs: they shall consume; into smoke shall they consume away. The wicked borroweth, and payeth not again: but the righteous sheweth mercy, and giveth. For such as be blessed of him shall inherit the earth; and they that be cursed of him shall be cut off. The steps of a good man are ordered by the Lord: and he delighteth in his way. Though he fall, he shall not be utterly cast down: for the Lord upholdeth him with his hand. I have been young, and now am old; yet have I not seen the righteous forsaken, nor his seed begging bread. He is ever merciful, and lendeth; and his seed is blessed. Depart from evil, and do good; and dwell for evermore. For the Lord loveth judgment, and forsaketh not his saints; they are preserved for ever: but the seed of the wicked shall be cut off. The righteous shall inherit the land, and dwell therein for ever. The mouth of the righteous speaketh wisdom, and his tongue talketh of judgment. The law of his God is in his heart; none of his steps shall slide. The wicked watcheth the righteous, and seeketh to slay him. The Lord will not leave him in his hand, nor condemn him when he is judged. Wait on the Lord, and keep his way, and he shall exalt thee to inherit the land: when the wicked are cut off, thou shalt see it. I have seen the wicked in great power, and spreading himself like a green bay tree. Yet he passed away, and, lo, he was not. yea, I sought him, but he could not be found. Mark the perfect man, and behold the upright: for the end of that man is peace. But the transgressors shall be destroyed together: the end of the wicked shall be cut off. But the salvation of the righteous is of the Lord: he is their strength in the time of trouble. And the Lord shall help them, and deliver them: he shall deliver them from the wicked, and save them, because they trust in him."

(7) Luke 4:28-30—**Unhurt even in harm's way:** *"And all they in the synagogue, when they heard these things, were filled with wrath, And rose up, and thrust him out of the city, and led him unto the brow of the hill whereon their city was built, that they might cast him down headlong. But he passing through the midst of them went his way."*

(8) Acts 12—**How to let God clear the record and level the fighting field:** *"Now about that time Herod the king stretched forth his hands to vex certain of the church. And he killed James the brother of John with the sword. And because he saw it pleased the Jews, he proceeded further to take Peter also. (Then were the days of unleavened bread.) And when he had apprehended him, he put him in prison, and delivered him to four quarternions of soldiers to keep him; intending after Easter to bring him forth to the people. Peter therefore was kept in prison: but prayer was made without ceasing of the church unto God for him. And when Herod would have brought him forth, the same night Peter was sleeping between two soldiers, bound with two chains: and the keepers before the door kept the prison. And, behold, the angel of the Lord came upon him, and a light shined in prison: and he smote Peter on the side, and raised him up, saying, Arise up quickly. And his chains fell off from his hands. And the angel said unto him, Gird thyself, and bind on thy sandals. And so he did. And he saith unto him, Cast thy garment about thee, and follow me. And he went out, and followed him; and wist not that it was true which was done by the angel; but thought he saw a vision. When they were past the first and the second ward, they came unto the iron gate that leadeth unto the city; which opened to them of his own accord: and they went out, and passed on through one street; and forthwith the angel departed from him. And when Peter was come to himself, he said, Now I know of a surety, that the Lord hath sent his angel, and hath delivered me out of the hand of Herod, and from all the expectation of the people of the Jews. And when he had considered the thing, he came to the house of Mary the mother of John, whose surname was Mark; where many were gathered together praying. And as Peter knocked at the door of the gate, a damsel came to hearken, named Rhoda. And when she knew Peter's voice, she opened not the gate for gladness, but ran in, and told how Peter stood before the gate. And they said unto her, Thou art mad. But she constantly affirmed that it was even so. Then said they, It is his angel. But Peter continued knocking: and when they had opened the door, and saw him, they were astonished. But he, beckoning unto them with the hand to hold their peace, declared unto them how the Lord had brought him out of the prison. And he said, Go shew these things unto James, and to the brethren. And he departed, and went into another place. Now as soon as it was day, there was no small*

stire among the soldiers, what was become of Peter. And when Herod had sought for him, and found him not, he examined the keepers, and commanded that they should be put to death. And he went down from Judaea to Caesarea, and there abode. And Herod was highly displeased with them of Tyre and Sidon: but they came with one accord to him, and having made Blastus the king's chamberlain their friend, desired peace; because their country was nourished by the king's country. And upon a set day Herod, arrayed in royal apparel, sat upon his throne, and made an oration unto them. And the people gave a shout, saying, it is the voice of a god, and not of a man. And immediately the angel of the Lord smote him, because he gave not God the glory; and he was eaten of worms, and gave up the ghost. But the word of God grew and multiplied. And Barnabas and Saul returned from Jerusalem, when they had fulfilled their ministry, and took with them John, whose surname was Mark."

(10) Ephesians 6:10-18—**Weapons for warriors in every war:** *"Finally, my brethren, be strong in the Lord, and in the power of his might. Put on the whole armour of God, that ye may be able to stand against the wiles of the devil. For we wrestle not against flesh and blood, but against principalities, against powers, against the rulers of the darkness of this world, against spiritual wickedness in high places. Wherefore take unto you the whole armour of God, that ye may be able to withstand in the evil day, and having done all, to stand. Stand therefore having your loins girt about with truth, and having on the breastplate of righteousness; And your feet shod with the preparation of the gospel of peace; Above all, taking the shield of faith, wherewith ye shall be able to quench all the fiery darts of the wicked. And take the helmet of salvation, and the sword of the spirit, which is the word of God: Praying always with all prayer and supplication in the Spirit, and watching thereunto with all perseverance and supplication for all saints."*

NOTES

NOTES

NOTES

NOTES

www.ingramcontent.com/pod-product-compliance
Lightning Source LLC
Chambersburg PA
CBHW032027230426
43671CB00005B/226